FISHING IN A SHALLOW SEA

FISHING IN A SHALLOW SEA

Church Strategies for the 21ˢᵗ Century

Rev. Dr. Michael S. Piazza

A SHALLOW SEA

The reality that, even in strong and healthy congregations, attendance, giving, volunteerism, and spiritual formation are less frequent and consistent, even among the devoted.

Come and follow me, and I will make you fishers of souls.
Matthew 4:19

TABLE OF CONTENTS

PREFACE

T raditional, mainline, or "vintage" churches are struggling to navigate and adapt to the exponential rate of change that technology has created in every sector of society. This change requires any institution to be agile in its structure, effective in its marketing and communication, engaging in its product or program offerings, and efficient in its use of technology if it wants to survive. None of these are typical of what are often called "old-line" churches. For this reason, many experts predict the continued decline and perhaps ultimate extinction of these congregations and denominations. While it is likely true that declining participation in traditional churches will continue, this project attempts to offer alternatives that might slow or, given adequate effort, even reverse this decline.

These methods have been tested in a typical mainline church that experienced decades of decline so severe that other "experts" encouraged the church to shutter.. Most of what is described began as experiments in this particular congregation. Given their positive impact, these methods were adapted to a consulting practice that presently works with dozens of congregations and several denominational judicatories. The ideas contained in this book also were used in a graduate academic course that was developed and taught at Hartford Seminary.

I am calling the setting in which mainline churches find themselves currently a "shallow sea." This descriptor includes trends like decreasing frequency of attendance, declining generosity, and the rise of the "nones" who do not identify with any denomination or tradition, and the "dones" who have left the church. The "sea" analogy also reflects the perils of rapid, continuous, and exponential change that creates a great challenge in anticipating and planning any institution's future, and that requires ever increasing adaptability and agility.

INTRODUCTION

I was licensed to preach in the United Methodist Church in June 1973. The previous year I served as the youth director in my home church in Statesboro, Georgia while I completed my freshman year in college. Two weeks after I received my license, the bishop appointed me to a circuit of three small, rural churches in middle Georgia. When he read my name and the name of the circuit to which I was assigned, he drolly observed that even I could not harm these churches, which dated back to the Revolutionary War.

As it turned out, the bishop was correct. Although I had turned only 19 in July and had no experience, no training, no education, and no business being a pastor, the churches flourished. One congregation grew sufficiently to be able to afford their own fulltime pastor after a year, while I remained as the pastor for the other two. That experience has been repeated during the more than four decades of my ministry since then. Although it would sound arrogant if I had said it aloud, my internal supposition at the time was that a new pastor went to a new church and the church grew. That was my experience with the seven congregations I served until 2011.

The Cathedral of Hope United Church of Christ grew rapidly and significantly during the two decades I was their pastor. When my denominational leadership asked me to consult with other congregations about renewal, I wasn't sure what I knew. For this reason, I agreed to become the pastor of Virginia-Highland Church UCC in Atlanta, Georgia in March 2011. They could not afford to pay a pastor, so they agreed to serve as a revitalization lab. Because their attendance was in the 20s, it seemed they had little to lose.

Virginia-Highland Church (VHC) taught me, rather abruptly, that churches do not grow automatically when they get a new pastor, even if that pastor has a positive track record for church growth. During my first year, I genuinely feared I had made a terrible mistake believing that the church could be revived, or that I had lost my skills for congregational renewal. The one thing that was apparent was that growing a church today is more difficult than it has been at any time since I began my ministry in 1973.

Although I worked fulltime as a consultant, no church I served received more passion and energy. The incremental results seemed to come at an excruciatingly slow pace. It wasn't until we installed a new database that I discovered that VHC was much bigger than I thought. We had almost 2,400 people in our system, a significant portion of whom considered that their church. The challenges were:

- There were virtually no 60-, 70-, or 80-year-old members,
- Most of the membership was in their 30s and 40s,
- They were not drawn from the neighborhood around the church but from all over the Atlanta area, and, most significantly,
- They attended less regularly than any congregation I had ever served.

The fact that even committed people attend worship one-third as often as their parents meant we had to grow three times as much even to notice. Because Virginia-Highland Church was essentially a new church start, and because it attracted a congregation that was much younger than the median age of most mainline churches, it became a microcosm of what is happening in the larger church and what all mainline churches are beginning to face. Put simply, the reduction in the **frequency** of attendance explains a significant portion of the decline that the church is facing. Discovering what caused the situation, the "shallow sea," if you will, probably kept me in ministry at a point when I had become overwhelmingly discouraged. It also motivated me to find solutions not only for that church, but also for others.

For this reason, I developed a graduate class for Hartford Seminary that identifies the sources of today's challenges but spends most of the class time discovering solutions that can keep churches thriving in a day when most of the news about the mainline church is depressingly bad. In addition, I have adapted what I have learned for the congregations and judicatories with which I consult. Ultimately, I have tried to document my work in this book..

Because my present ministry is multi-faceted, this book draws from several different areas. I am the founder and president of Agile Church Consulting, a vocational coach for eight to 10 pastors, a church technology specialist, a professor, a pastor, and an author. The project attempts to share how I, in these varying roles, have experienced and adapted to the shallow sea reality of churches and denominations. What follows is an effort to describe how the dynamics of exponential social change impact the mainline church and, more importantly, an effort to offer seminal prescriptions for maintaining vitality in this time of transition.

The truth is church attendance will continue to decline, and many historic churches will close. Denominations will continue to shrink and consolidate. However, none of this signals the demise of the Christian faith or the Church of Jesus Christ. We must find new ways to express and experience faith that are congruent with the rapid rate of change that spreads us all too thin. Although this book makes no pretense to be the ultimate solution, it is a snapshot of a moment in this great transition that might offer some hope to those who are willing to remain agile and adaptive.

THE CHALLENGE WE FACE

F ew would argue the tenet that mainline denominational churches in the United States are generally in a season of decline.

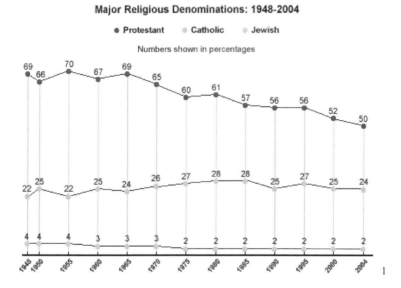

Major Religious Denominations: 1948-2004

● Protestant   ○ Catholic   ○ Jewish

Numbers shown in percentages

Many factors have been offered to explain this decline, but I believe, however, that much of the diagnosis and, hence, many of the remedies miss key points.

A New Normal

America is returning to a "new normal." In other words, the panic about decline is caused, in part, by comparing the current state of the church to

[1] Linda Lyons, "Tracking U.S. Religious Preferences Over the Decades," Gallup, http://news.gallup.com/poll/16459/tracking-us-religious-preferences-over-decades.aspx, (May 24, 2005)

an anomalous time, rather than a more traditional state of the church in America.

In their book *The Churching of America, 1776-1990*, professors Roger Finke and Rodney Starke contend that, since colonial days, the United States has gone "from a nation in which most people took no part in organized religion to a nation in which nearly two-thirds of American adults do."[2] Re-examining historical statistics for church membership, Professors Finke and Starke concluded that 17 percent of the population were "religious adherents" in 1776; 37 percent in 1860; 53 percent in 1916; 59 percent in 1952; and 62 percent in 1980.[3]

Rather than viewing current attendance and membership trends with such great panic, perhaps we might find a better approach by looking at historic trends that long have seen these factors as cyclical.

Changing Gender Roles

A second factor that has been ignored for too long but become apparent in studying the local history of numerous congregations, is changing gender roles. It also deserves much greater academic attention than can be offered here. It generally is accepted that the apex of congregational vitality in America occurred after World War II. This is explained in part by the population increase from baby boomers, which peaked in the late 1950s and early '60s.

In reading the history of local congregations, however, what becomes apparent is that, in many cases, churches often launched significant new programs, ministries, and building programs shortly after the war. Women who had found new roles in business and industry were displaced as men returned home. These women often went to their local church where they used their newly-found skills to lead the congregation in a season of renewal. This period of greatest vitality began to diminish as more and more women entered the workforce and gave less of their time and skills to the local church.

---

[2] Roger Finke and Rodney Stark, *The Churching of America, 1776-1990* (New Jersey: Rutgers University Press, 1992), 1

[3] Ibid., 16

This was illustrated clearly in the rise and fall of Virginia-Highland Church (United Church of Christ) in Atlanta, Georgia. Reading their history, and knowing a few of those surviving women, led to a closer examination of the history and patterns in other Protestant churches. While mainline Protestantism benefited from an increased number of women clergy, the loss of so many skilled women volunteers contributed to the loss of vitality in many congregations.

Decreasing Frequency of Attendance

Although there are many other factors that deserve our attention, there is one that has been most impactful and largely neglected. Many churches have virtually the same number of members and level of satisfaction, but their attendance, giving, and participation have diminished substantially. It is simply a matter of the decreasing **frequency** of attendance.

Dr. Thom S. Rainer is the president and CEO of LifeWay Christian Resources, a former professor at The Southern Baptist Theological Seminary, and the founding dean of the Billy Graham School of Missions and Evangelism. He summarizes the problem most succinctly in a web article entitled "The Number One Reason for the Decline in Church Attendance." He bluntly offers an assessment that should be obvious but that has seldom been observed:

Stated simply, the number one reason for the decline in church attendance is that members attend with less frequency than they did just a few years ago. Allow me to explain. If the frequency of attendance changes, then attendance will respond accordingly. For example, if 200 members attend every week the average attendance is, obviously, 200. But if one-half of those members miss only one out of four weeks, the attendance drops to 175.

Did you catch that? No members left the church. Everyone is still relatively active in the church. But attendance declined over 12 percent because half the members changed their attendance behavior slightly.

This phenomenon can take place rather quickly in an individual church. And leaders in the church are often left scratching their heads because the behavioral change is so slight, almost imperceptible. We really don't notice when someone who attends four times a month

3

begins to attend only three times a month. Nor do we typically catch it when the twice-a-month attendee becomes a once-a-month attendee.[4]

Gallup's tracking of church attendance supports what most pastors have observed. Even our most active members attend less frequently.

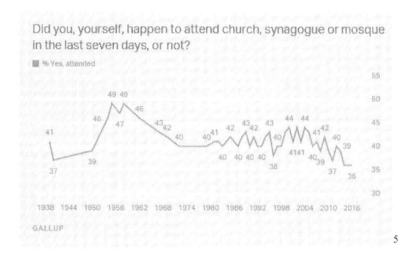

Did you, yourself, happen to attend church, synagogue or mosque in the last seven days, or not?

[5]

Rainer's other premise about a decline in attendance while membership remains stable is supported by a 2015 Pew Research Report that observed that, by and large, Americans' attitudes toward and value of religion remain relatively unchanged. Most mainline congregations, however, are declining at a rate that belies that reality.

---

[4] Thom S. Rainer, "The Number One Reason for the Decline in Church Attendance and Five Ways to Address It," http://thomrainer.com/2013/08/the-number-one-reason-for-the-decline-in-church-attendance-and-five-ways-to-address-it/, (August 19, 2013)

[5] Frank Newport, "Five Key Findings on Religion in the U.S.", Gallup, http://news.gallup.com/poll/200186/five-key-findings-religion.aspx, (December 23, 2016)

Number of Religiously Affiliated Americans Saying Religion 'Very Important' to Them Holds Steady

	2007	2014	Change
Number of adults in U.S.	227.2m	244.8m	+17.6m
Share of adults who are religiously affiliated	83.1%	76.5%	-6.6 points
NUMBER of religiously affiliated adults	188.8m	187.3m	-1.5m
Share of affiliated adults saying religion is "very important" in their lives	64.5%	65.5%	+1 point
NUMBER of religiously affiliated adults saying religion is "very important" in their lives	121.8m	122.7m	+0.9m

Source: 2014 Religious Landscape Study, conducted June 4-Sept. 30, 2014.
PEW RESEARCH CENTER

6

A large part of this disparity was explained in 2005 by sociologists C. Kirk Hadaway and Penny Long Marler in "The Journal for the Scientific Study of Religion" and reported by Kelly Shattuck for ChurchLeaders.com. They discovered that, contrary to what 40 percent of people reported, statistical evidence shows that only 17.7 percent of Americans attend church each week.[7] That is a decline of more than 50 percent and is supported by the realities that most vintage churches are now experiencing in their pews. Shattuck writes:

What Hadaway and Marler, along with Mark Chaves, author of the "National Congregations Study," discovered was at play is what researchers call "the halo effect"—the difference between what people tell pollsters and what people actually do. Americans tend to

[6]"America's Changing Religious Landscape," http://www.pewforum.org/2015/05/12/americas-changing-religious-landscape/, Pew Research Center, (May 12, 2015)

[7] Kelly Shattuck, "7 Startling Facts: An Up Close Look at Church Attendance in America," Church Leaders, https://churchleaders.com/pastors/pastor-articles/139575-7-startling-facts-an-up-close-look-at-church-attendance-in-america.html, (December 14, 2017)

over-report socially desirable behavior like voting and attending church and under-report socially undesirable behavior like drinking.

Gallup Poll Editor in Chief Frank Newport agrees that the halo effect factors into poll results. During a Gallup telephone survey of a random sampling of about 1,000 Americans nationwide, interviewers ask respondents questions such as, "In the last seven days, did you attend a church service, excluding weddings and funerals?" to determine their church-going habits. "When people try to reconstruct their own behavior, particularly more frequently occurring on-and-off behavior, it is more difficult, especially in a telephone interview scenario," Newport says. But he stands behind Gallup's 40 percent figure: "I've been reviewing [U.S. church attendance] carefully," he says. "No matter how we ask the question to people, we get roughly 40 percent of Americans who present themselves as regular church attendees." He adds, however, that if you were to freeze the United States on any Sunday morning, you may find fewer than 40 percent of the country's adults actually in churches.[8]

Of course, decreasing frequency in attendance also means declining revenues, volunteers, and influence. This likely will increase as the church passes into the hands of generations who never lived in a culture in which regular church attendance was normative. The increasing percentage of the population that does not have any religious affiliation (the "rise of the 'nones'" as it is known) will only accelerate this trend.[9]

Assuming that Dr. Rainey and thousands of panicked pastors are correct that this is the number one challenge traditional churches face, I hope to articulate some of the root causes and offer some approaches that can enhance the future vitality of a "vintage church," a term I use for a traditional/mainline church.

---

[8] Ibid.

[9] Michael Lipka, "A closer look at America's rapidly growing religious 'nones'," Pew Research, http://www.pewresearch.org/fact-tank/2015/05/13/a-closer-look-at-americas-rapidly-growing-religious-nones/, (May 13, 2005)

A SHALLOW SEA CONGREGATION

There are several ways to approach how we might respond to the "shallow sea" phenomenon, but let me begin by saying that the title is in no way meant to be pejorative toward those who attend church less frequently. It does not imply that they are shallow people nor that their faith is less profound or "deep." Rather, it is simply a descriptor that our work as leaders is likely to be much wider ranging and, thus, less deep. For example, when people attend worship less frequently it becomes difficult to go deeply into a topic through a sermon series. Unless your congregation is comprised almost entirely of seniors, it is likely that half the younger members were not present for last week's sermon. Relationships, too, cannot be built entirely on Sundays because people simply are not there.

Describing any congregation in a book is always risky. As a living organism, presenting a movie rather than a photograph would be preferable, if that was possible. Some congregations have been so effective at resisting change, however, that the movie would need to be viewed in slow motion or stop-action. Such is not the case with churches that will survive long into the 21st century. Thriving churches are likely to have many different styles, theologies, and expressions of their faith, but the one thing they will have in common is an ability to adapt their message and ministry in an everchanging climate and culture.

Change and church often have been mutually exclusive. What follows, however, is the story of one congregation that I intend to serve as a parable for some hope for future vintage churches. For decades, Virginia-Highland Church epitomized mainline decline in every way. As its neighborhood changed during the 1980s and '90s, long-term members moved away and left the church. Shortly after the turn of the 21st century, the fortunes of the Virginia-Highland neighborhood reversed. Property values remained strong, even through the most recent recession, and the neighborhood was named the "Best Overall Neighborhood" in Atlanta in 2011 by readers of "Creative Loafing," an alternative weekly newspaper.

In June 2011, "Atlanta Magazine" designated Virginia-Highland its "favorite neighborhood overall."[1]

I became senior pastor of the church that bears the neighborhood's name in March 2011. After serving for two decades at what became one of the largest progressive and inclusive congregations in the South, being called to serve a church with no resources, few people, and a dim future came as a bit of a shock. The Cathedral of Hope United Church of Christ (CoH) in Dallas, Texas had grown from a couple hundred members to several thousand during the years that I was there. At its peak, weekly attendance was more than 2,200 and the annual budget more than $4.5 million.

When I arrived at Virginia-Highland Church (VHC) the average attendance at morning worship was 26, which was smaller than my staff meetings at the Cathedral of Hope. VHC had no endowment, and they were unable to pay a pastor. Had it not been for a preschool that rented space in the church's education building for 15 years, they would have been forced to close a decade or so before my arrival. The building had deteriorated greatly due to deferred maintenance. The few younger members were mostly holding on to care for the few older women who once had been the core of the church's strength and vitality. Judicatory officials twice had recommended the congregation close and the valuable property be sold.

When I went to VHC, with four decades of pastoral experience, I had some clear expectations. Most of the churches I had served grew relatively quickly. Virginia-Highland Church was a rude awakening. There was an almost immediate doubling of attendance, but then, for the next 18 months, it seemed that nothing I tried was making much difference. Attendance and giving ticked up but not enough to make the church viable. My spouse and I discussed the distinct possibility that we had made a mistake and that this church really didn't have a future. Privately, I considered that the shelf-life of my own gifts and experience had expired.

---

[1]Amanda Heckert, ed., "Hot 'Hoods," *Atlanta Magazine*, https://web.archive.org/web/20110930085606/http://www.atlantamagazine.com/features/neighborhoods/home.aspx, (June 2011)

When they interviewed me about becoming their pastor, someone asked why I would come to VHC considering they weren't paying me and I could make a good salary in many other places. My answer was a bit blunt and lacking in spirituality, but I told them frankly that it was because I thought VHC was a "good franchise." By that, I meant that their location, history, facility, and values made them a good candidate to be a strong church in that particular location in Atlanta.

As the church failed to respond to all my efforts and theirs in that first year, however, I was forced to reevaluate many of my presumptions about what had led to congregational renewal in the past. Harder still, I was forced to recognize mistakes I had made. One of the maxims that recommends planning is that mistakes are much less expensive on paper than in real life. The least expensive way, of course, is to let someone else make the mistakes and then learn from them. For that reason, it might be helpful to share some of our mistakes.

My Arrogance

After being the pastor of a church that grew to more than 4,000 members, I arrogantly presumed I could pastor a small church like VHC while working a very demanding second job. "After all," I joked, "we had more tenors in the choir at CoH than VHC has members."

What that missed was, well, everything. Writing a sermon takes the same amount of time whether it will be heard by 25 or 2,500. The sermons I had been preaching to the world's largest lesbian, gay, bisexual, and transgender congregation in Texas weren't transferable to a small, diverse congregation in Georgia. In the Dallas church more than 150 people were involved in producing worship every week, but now it was just me and a couple of very part-time staff members. Creating a powerful and transformational worship experience each week without resources required extraordinary creativity and effort.

Visitors were not impressed by our building that was in disrepair, nor our music program with an old organ that frequently shorted out. My spouse was a one-man hospitality committee, altar guild, and greeting ministry. The bylaws required congregational approval for any expenditure of more than $500, so roof leaks, failed water heaters, damaged walls, and even marketing opportunities all required a congregational meeting to approve. The effort required to renew VHC in the first year or so exceeded anything I had ever experienced, largely because of an encrustation of controlling administration. The bylaws were 27 pages long and entirely fear-based and controlling.

Personal Relationships

In addition, I missed the fact that, while much pastoral work can be done from anywhere, there is no replacing relationships and presence. My consulting work kept me on a plane and out of town at least half the time, and, unlike megachurches, smaller congregations require personal interactions and community building.

Much of what is written here will stress how to use technology and other modern tools to "fish in a shallow sea." It should be noted, however, that community and connection are great gifts that the church offers and that our society profoundly needs. It is fascinating that, at a time when people are increasingly isolated in their own digitally-screened-off worlds, there is a greater and greater value for public space. Businesses like Starbucks have built a successful business model by become people's "third place" or "new front porch."[2]

Simply attracting people to listen to well-crafted sermons is not enough to renew a church. Having led what was technically a megachurch for several years, I missed the significance of creating meaningful experiences of connection and community. As the leaders of many renowned churches can attest, you cannot build a heathy congregation with visitors. We needed programs that would transform "tourists" into pilgrims. We needed opportunities for a community drawn from all over the metropolitan area to connect with one another and to identify and commit to a common vision.

Growing vs. Reversing Decline

---

[2] Alison Overholt, "Do You Hear What Starbucks Hears?", *Fast Company,* https://www.fastcompany.com/50607/do-you-hear-what-starbucks-hears, (July 1, 2004)

The third reality I missed was that growing a strong small congregation is considerably easier than reversing a long season/tradition/identity of decline. I once advised a pastor considering a call that, "Giving birth is much easier than raising the dead." VHC, like many other declining churches, had embraced the idea of inevitable decline, and saw themselves as a faithful remnant of their values and identity. The vision of the church as seen through the lens of long-term members could not have been more different than the church new people thought they were visiting.

Many years ago, I read that a single train engine rolling 10 miles an hour can break through several feet of concrete. However, a train that is sitting still can be immobilized by a two-inch block of wood placed in front of its wheels. While that illustration is difficult to verify, it is very clear that momentum is a powerful force, and, when a church has none, getting it to move forward is almost impossible. A new/young church energized by vision can grow through early developmental stages, but an older congregation seeking to return to viability usually requires much more energy and resources than are available to them.

Change

The most important mistake also was the most difficult to identify. The world had changed dramatically since I arrived to renew the Cathedral of Hope in 1987, which then experienced phenomenal growth. What worked in congregational renewal for years then no longer worked, or at least not in the ways it once did.

We all probably are frustrated when churches refuse to try new things and learn new lessons. Honesty compels me to admit, however, that it took more than a year of failure and frustration before I recognized that what I always had done and what always had worked simply was no longer effective and that I needed to change my ways of leading. The most difficult person to persuade that a change must be made is often the leader you see in a mirror. This is especially true when that leader has known historic success in the past. Ironically, it was only when I heard myself say to a denominational bureaucrat, "When the horse is dead, dismount," that I realized that truth also applied to me.

Once I realized that, to be an effective church leader in the 21st century, I was going to have to learn new skills, my attitude moved almost immediately from despair and self-doubt to excitement and anticipation. Learning something new always has been a challenge I have enjoyed, and I had an opportunity to reinvent myself yet again and learn new skills after doing essentially the same job since I was 18 years old.

Because Virginia-Highland Church had been dying for some time, they acknowledged they had nothing to lose, so, together, we began to experiment with what a 21st-century "vintage church" might look like. It also became necessary for me to shift my expectations. After 40 years of preaching, and gaining some reputation for that skill, I found myself having to learn how to preach visually to people who see the whole world through a tiny computer in their hands. We had to develop new metrics for what it means to be a thriving church, new systems and structures that better matched contemporary lifestyles, needs, and giving patterns. VHC caught a new vision of itself and discovered a new mission in its community. Suddenly, the breath of Life began to return to what had been dry bones, and almost 300 people showed up for Easter worship.

Today, although still a small-to-medium-size church, VHC has quintupled worship attendance, its budget, and its community outreach. It has an outsized million-dollar program for the homeless. Colleagues who attended worship rated it among the best and most authentically diverse in a city filled with churches. We restored the building and made it accessible. It is a thriving community of faith with a very bright future that includes children and an almost century-old member who is present almost every Sunday.

It took much more time and effort than any church I have pastored. In my third year there I was still very frustrated by Sunday morning attendance. I had expected it to break 200 that year, but we were still short of that. Some Sundays I was grateful to break 100. Giving and volunteer ministry were remarkably strong for a church so small, but, despite what I thought was high-quality worship, attendance lagged behind any of the eight churches I had pastored. One Sunday morning, as I listened to the choir singing an African-American spiritual, the congregation spontaneously rose to their feet and began to sway and clap along. That was a first, considering the services were fairly liturgical. Still, it felt right and was a sign that the church truly had begun to change.

As I looked around at those gathered that day and tried to access the wonderful dynamic, I suddenly realized that I was one of the oldest people in the room. Miss Blanche, who has been a member of that church for almost a century, was there, but there was almost no one between her age and mine. The church was utterly without 60-, 70-, and 80-year-olds. It was then that it hit me that we were missing the generation of members who do most of the volunteering, giving, and consistent worshipping in most vintage churches in America. No wonder we were struggling with some of that. We had accomplished what most churches say is their goal. We had attracted a young and diverse congregation. A survey on a Sunday in 2017 revealed the following demographics:

Average age:	42.04
Gender:	51% male, 47% female, 2% transgender
Avg. distance to church:	7.3 miles
Length of membership:	4 years, 1 month
Members:	53% of those present
Race:	67% white, 22% African American, 7% Hispanic 2% Asian

The average age of the congregation provided a significant clue to our attendance challenge, which was driven home the following week when we installed the new church database. It reported that we had more than 2,200 people connected with the church in some way. At first, I thought this was a mistake. Surely the church didn't have that many people who had given us their information and were connected to our church in some way. A check with our administrator revealed that it was no mistake and that this was an accurate record of those who had attended, registered their presence with us, and provided contact information. Although our weekly attendance had grown excruciatingly slowly, the "sea" that constituted Virginia-Highland Church was very wide. That was confirmed by standing-room-only crowds on Easter, even though fully half of the youthful regular congregation went home to be with their families on that Sunday.

A study of VHC's demographics and attendance patterns revealed that they are less than half the age of the typical mainline church in which more than 60 percent of the membership is 60 or older.[3] While many churches seek a consultant to help them discern how to attract young couples with children, that church struggled with the downside of a congregation comprised almost entirely of such a demographic. The majority of VHC's members are part of a generation that attends worship much less frequently. This dynamic forced them to struggle with how to do church when at least 50 percent of the congregation is different each week, and with what church means when regular worship has a different value. During the six-and-a-half years I served there the oldest member, Miss Blanche, was one of less than a handful of people who had worship attendance that exceeded 80 percent of the Sundays.

VHC had to discover its own compelling vision, develop new technology to sustain stewardship, find new metrics to measure vitality, and use technology and social media to encourage attendance and remain connected to new and younger members. All of this will be discussed in greater detail, but it is important to understand that this approach to church was not developed in some seminary lab, but in a very real congregation that had declined to the point of being pronounced dead by its own denomination. Virginia-Highland Church's renewal happened with absolutely no financial resources. What they had was willingness to experiment with what a new future might look like for them. That sense of adventure is all too rare in the church, which may be the main reason few congregations actually experience the renewal they almost unanimously claim to desire.

---

[3] Michael Lipka, "Which U.S. religious groups are oldest and youngest?," Pew Research, http://www.pewresearch.org/fact-tank/2016/07/11/which-u-s-religious-groups-are-oldest-and-youngest, (July 11, 2016)

A BIBLE A HYMNAL, AND A DATABASE

O nce upon a time, circuit-riding preachers traveled the countryside from one small congregation to another, riding on horseback and carrying a Bible and a hymnal. Today, preachers can travel lighter with the Bible and hymnal on their smartphone, tablet, or laptop. What must be added to every effective church leader's toolbox is an effective database that they understand and use.

More than having a contact management system, though, the church must learn how to use it effectively to communicate, to connect, and to create community. Vital, growing churches who are attracting a new generation of members will have more people who come less frequently, so the growth may seem almost invisible without very careful, deliberate, and consistent record keeping, connection, and strategic communication. This is an essential tool for fishing in a broader but shallower sea.

Every effective company and organization does everything possible to capture a person's information so they can connect with them. This is one area in which churches have failed to heed Jesus' admonition to "be as cunning as a serpent, but as innocent as a dove."[1] This instruction was offered as Jesus sent his disciples out as evangelists and healers. The church must be cunning in how it learns to stay connected with people who come to worship less frequently, are scattered geographically, would be resistant to visits, and have short attention spans because they are inundated with information.

Companies are willing to give away a car just to garner people's contact information, but most churches let people come and go without ever learning or retaining their names.

An effective database begins with a thoughtful and effective strategy for collecting people's information. Through a series of experiments, Virginia-Highland Church managed to get almost 90 percent of those present to register their attendance.

---

[1] Mt. 10:16 ISV.

Michael S. Piazza

We did this by asking *everyone* in the room to register their attendance in a pad that was passed down the aisle. Visitors were not singled out because everyone was registering.

We welcomed people at the start of the service and told visitors that they were our guests. We promised not to embarrass them in any way. The ONLY thing that was asked of them was to share their physical and email addresses at the time of the offering, later in the service. They were told exactly what we would do with the information: we would write to them and invite them to come back, as well as send them information about the church. Then, at that moment in the service, we asked everyone to register their attendance and reminded guests that we wanted them to give us their physical address so we could write to them and their email address so we could keep in touch.

Regular attenders were encouraged to consider themselves as hosts, so they, too, would register their attendance, which made guests feel more comfortable about doing likewise.

Sunday registration was how we kept track of people who missed three, five, and 10 Sundays in a row. Even if we knew that someone was present but simply didn't register their attendance, we sent them a "Miss You" email after three weeks to let them know that we took registration seriously. This was the only way to keep in touch with new people who attended infrequently and might not have been missed until they were long gone.

A volunteer collected the registration forms after worship each Sunday, and someone was assigned to send first-time visitors an email that afternoon. Another very reliable volunteer or volunteers came in on Monday to input all the information. That volunteer then sent the deacons (pastoral care team) a list of those who had missed three Sundays in a row, and the staff a list of those who had missed five Sundays in a row. We had a strategy for reaching out to both groups, which, generally, was by email. At times, though, we sent cards. If a person had missed nine or more Sundays they were called. In older congregations, in which people attend worship more regularly and sit in the same place, this may not seem needed. It is the only way, however, to begin to build a new and younger congregation because "visitors" are seldom missed until it is too late.

A ministry should be put in place to reach out to a first-time visitor without singling them out during worship or embarrassing them. A record also should be made of their visit. Initially, they may give you only their name, but when they return, and finally do give you more complete information, you don't want to send them a first-time visitor packet without acknowledging that you know this was not their first time to worship with you.

As noted earlier, people do not attend nearly as frequently as they think they do. A gentle contact from the church can help combat that. After a time, people begin to let the church staff know ahead of time when they are going to miss several Sundays because they know they will be contacted otherwise. Creating that expectation of regular attendance in a new and younger generation is critical in a culture with so many things competing for their attention on Sunday mornings.

Even smaller churches need to offer gathering times that are alternatives to Sunday morning. A database will be critical to keeping the entire congregation connected. Organizations pay huge sums to buy mailing lists to use for fundraising. Churches too often allow those valuable assets to slip through their fingers.

A good database should allow members to access their own records to check their giving, update their information, upload a photograph, and create connections. It also will allow people to email one another without having to give out personal information.

One of the critical functions of a database or, more accurately, a "church management system" is to keep track of volunteer hours. Most churches give away tens of thousands of dollars in service to those in need and to the community they serve. The problem is, without keeping track of those hours, you cannot report to the congregation, community, or granting agencies just how much good you do.

There are hundreds of church management systems available that range in cost from only $50 a month to a $250,000 flat fee. The most effective one is the one you use. The time when one or two people kept a congregation's information on an Excel spreadsheet has passed. An effective pastor will want to know who was missing every Sunday. We invest tremendous energy and resources in Sunday morning worship and those who are present. The vital future church will have to create an equally effective ministry for keeping in touch with those who are not.

By the time I left, Virginia-Highland Church had somewhere around 300 members, and about half that number regularly attended worship. That wouldn't be unusual except at least half of those present each week were not members, at least not in the sense that they attended a class and formally joined. In addition, VHC's database recorded almost 2,500 people who had attended and given their information. Most of those 2,500 considered VHC their church, though they may have attended only once or twice a year. Many volunteered and gave much more frequently than they were present for worship. We tried to treat them the same as those who were present on Sunday, though they were a "virtual" congregation.

Ultimately, they are the overwhelming majority of the congregation, and churches must learn better how to be their church, too. As senior members of your church pass away, this will be more and more true for your congregation. Building your future "virtual" congregation will not happen by accident but will require a significant shift in thinking on behalf of church leaders. When a pastor looks out at the congregation on Sunday morning they think of them as the church. That same pastor needs to look at their database on Monday and think of the rest of their church and how to minister to and with them.

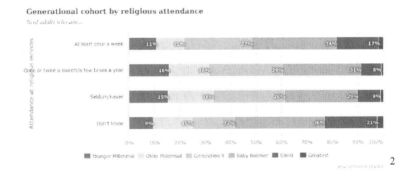

Generational cohort by religious attendance

2

2   "Religious   Landscape   Study: Attendance   at   religious   services," http://www.pewforum.org/religious-landscape-study/attendance-at-religious-services/, Pew Research Center

NEW METRICS FOR VITALITY

S uggesting that we measure church vitality by new metrics assumes, of course, that churches are measuring their vitality at all. It has been my experience that what we measure tends to grow, or, perhaps more accurately, what we fail to measure languishes without accurate information and resources. Almost every church tracks giving because expenditures, including the staff's salaries, depend on that. The result is most churches have stewardship programs, pledge drives, and software designed to increase financial support. Many churches measure membership, and a few churches design strategies for strengthening and increasing that metric. Church membership has diminished in meaning in congregations in which fewer and fewer active participants actually become official members. Attendance is the other metric used, though few churches study trends or do much to have an impact on what is happening until the downward trend is firmly established.

Membership, giving, and attendance each are vital signs of health that deserve our attention. With membership having decreased meaning, however, and giving and attendance becoming increasingly irregular, healthy churches must find additional ways to have an impact, ways that can be measured, reported, celebrated, and reinforced. The three traditional metrics are internally-focused, and, when reported on the back of a bulletin or church newsletter, they clearly are designed for those inside the church. They measure a church's ability to attract, and, although that is valuable and, in many ways, vital, there may be equally critical new metrics for a new day.

The need for new metrics is the premise of the book *The Externally Focused Church* by Rick Rusaw and Eric Swanson. They suggest that churches must shift their *raison d'etre*, moving from an internal focus for survival to an external focus for service, a tectonic shift for most mainline churches.[1]

---

[1] Rick Rusaw and Eric Swanson, *The Externally Focused Church,* (Loveland, CO: Group Publishing, 2004)

Michael S. Piazza

Reggie McNeal, in his book *Missional Renaissance* suggests that the church needs new "score cards," or new ways of measuring success and vitality. Attendance and giving will remain important, but he suggests that we must shift our thinking from the church as a destination to which people are attracted to understanding the church as a connection point from which people are sent to do the work of mission.[2]

This shift from attractional to incarnational is something many church leaders would agree with; however almost no churches measure and quantify how that happens. If what is measured grows then this is a serious neglect. In a grant application written while I was the senior pastor, it became necessary for Virginia-Highland Church to quantify its expenditures on mission, specifically on helping the homeless. Although this is a major missional priority, a look at the church budget would not reveal that. There was not a single dollar in the budget that was designated for the homeless, at least not apparently. One might conclude that saying we care about the homeless and not having anything in the budget for that work was hypocritical at best. Fortunately, the church understood the vitality of that mission needed to be measured in other ways.

Specifically, we looked at various ministries that were conducted largely with in-kind donations and volunteer energy. For example, we provided dinner twice a month for a homeless shelter. That ministry was nowhere to be seen in the budget; however, by tracking the number of volunteers who participated in preparing and serving each meal, and giving those volunteer hours a monetary value assigned by the Center for Nonprofit Management (or even minimum wage), we were able to demonstrate that, with this single ministry, the congregation was providing more than $50,000 worth of service to the homeless. The value of the meals also could be calculated by tracking the number of people fed during a year. We began to count the clothes donated, cases of bottled water, emergency food bags, sanitation kits, meals served, rent paid, shelter offered, etc. By using the database to track and quantify these volunteer contributions, we soon discovered that the total of the services

[2] Reggie McNeal, *Missional Renaissance: Changing the Scorecard for the Church*, (San Francisco: Jossey-Bass, 2009) 45

provided to the homeless was greater than our entire annual budget. Within the budget, we began to break out the amount of time staff spent conducting, directing, encouraging, and supporting these ministries. That portion of salaries was identified and added to our church's total donation.

The picture that emerged of the amount of service the church provided just to the homeless of Atlanta suddenly became clearer and much more tangible. This qualified us for a $1 million donation. It also reinforced the church's identity in living out its mission with integrity. Celebrating and honoring those who do this work encouraged more and more people to become involved. It now is not unusual for people to participate in ministry even though they may not attend worship. If we counted their presence only in a pew we would miss the greater picture of the church's true vitality.

Many churches give away as much in mission as they take up in offerings. They may also have as many people engaged in doing the mission of the church as they do in attendance. Unfortunately, few churches use their database to report and track this and calculate its value. How much is the space given away for use by other groups worth?

Throughout my career, it has been my practice to hold a ministry fair on one or two Sundays a year. They are designed to give people the opportunity to learn more about the church's various ministries and, perhaps, to sign up to support them. That is fairly common in most churches; what is not, however, is investing equal energy in ascertaining the "ministries" people are engaged in beyond the church. What are they doing because of who they are as people of faith? What boards do they serve on; where do they volunteer or give; who are they helping? Foster parents, voter registrars, fundraisers for the local public school, fair-trade product support, and dozens of other things should be reported, recorded, and celebrated.

The impact of many churches is so much greater than even they know. By measuring mission in this way, members begin to recognize that the church should be their "charity of choice," because it is doing the most at the lowest cost of any charity in town.

Michael S. Piazza

Knowing this, millennials may prove to be the most generous generation yet,[3] but they are not motivated by the idea of "meeting the budget" or making a pledge. They want to "spend" their time and money in places that have impact. The church may well be that place, but, because we do not measure it, report it, and celebrate it, no one knows.

In traditional congregations the "heroes" whose names people know often are the managers of the church. Quantifying and celebrating external ministries means making heroes of those who serve others. That shift—from internal heroes who serve the church to external heroes who ARE the church—changes everything. If all we measure and report, though, is the money given to the church and those who worship, it sends a clear message about how we define "church" and what is important.

Make no mistake: worship and generosity are important. Too often, though, the church becomes a machine that generates just enough power to run the machine. In a culture in which people have gone to church their entire lives, that might suffice, but, when that generation is gone, the machine can be shut off and sold. We must find new ways of measuring and celebrating the impact the church can and does have if we are going to attract a new generation that wants to find a community that matters.

To make the shift from an attractional to an incarnational community many churches will need to dramatically rethink their ideas of governance. We must shift our energy and resources from management and meetings to ministry and service. Becoming a permission-giving organism, rather than a bureaucratic, controlling organization, is inconceivable in many settings. "Congregationalism" is used too often as an excuse for more meetings and less action.

This is another area in which new metrics are required. For the most part, our understanding of congregationalism remains rooted in history but is entirely detached from our present reality. The concept of congregationalism to which most of our churches cling was formed in a time when villages and towns gathered in a meeting house and decided almost every issue the community faced. It was perhaps the purest and most idealized form of democracy our country ever knew, though women

---

[3] Andre Bourque, "Are Millennials the Most Generous Generation?", *Entrepreneur*, https://www.entrepreneur.com/article/271466, (March 29, 2016)

and people of color were not allowed to vote and often only those who owned property made the decisions. One might never know by its tenacious practice in the local church that this form of governance was relatively rare and, ultimately, short lived. Of course, the United States is a republic in which our governance is not determined by every citizen voting on every issue but by elected representatives. Today, the citizenry votes only on the highest officials and most dramatically significant issues.

Pure democracy worked (for some) when there was a citizenry with the capacity to be fully informed and completely invested in the outcome. Today, with the onslaught of information, that reality has changed dramatically, it is impossible to have a truly informed opinion about more than one or two issues beyond our work and family.

As I often say, "Pooled ignorance is not an asset." Even for our ancestors, with the growth of a nation and the complexity of society, fewer and fewer people were able to keep themselves adequately informed on the challenges facing their community. They selected wise men (and eventually women) and asked them to lead and to ensure that systems ran smoothly and that people's needs were met. These leaders were answerable to the people but were otherwise empowered to do the work that was needed for the common good.

By and large, most of our churches have followed that evolution of democracy. The congregation meets to make major decisions, express their will, and elect those who will lead. In the intervening time, wise women and men ensure that systems run smoothly and that people's needs are met. This is especially true in larger and growing congregations. The complexity and fluidity of those bodies make it impossible for everyone to be informed enough to make the decisions needed on a daily, weekly, and monthly basis.

In many small and/or declining congregations, however, there remains a value that every decision be made by the congregation, or at least approved by them. Although this would be perfect if we lived in an ideal world, it often proves to be a tyrannical illusion. The average worker in America today has less leisure time than any previous generation. Between work and family obligations, only a very small group within the church has adequate time to be involved enough to have an informed opinion about any area of the church other than the one or two in which they and their family are involved. The result often is the church is led by people who are painfully over-extended or, more often, those who are cut off from power in other areas of their lives, so they exert it at church in ways that are seldom healthy or helpful.

The speed at which the average person is living means that all too often a small group of the same people makes the same kinds of decisions year after year. Either the church declines to the point where that small group composes the congregation or new people never feel they actually belong to the church unless they get involved in management. In busy lives, it is almost always a choice. They can be involved in ministry that gives their lives meaning, or they can be involved in management that gives them a sense of inclusion. Beyond small or declining churches, true and full congregationalism is increasingly illusory. Healthy people almost always choose to spend their limited time with family and in meaningful ministry rather than church management.

Many years ago, I went to a new church that was deeply conflicted and rapidly declining. I was brand new and, thus, had no responsibility for the present condition of the congregation. I knew, however, that I had to act fast if the church was to be saved. One week, early on, fully 10 percent of the congregation made appointments with me to complain. They wanted to educate me about what I needed to do to fix the mess they had made. My breaking point came when I went to get my hair cut and my hair dresser began to tell me all the things I needed to do. When he took a breath, I launched into a long tirade about all the things he needed to do to cut hair better and run his business more effectively. Finally, I said, "You know, I've been getting my hair cut all my life but that doesn't qualify me to tell you how to do your job or run your shop, does it? So, why do you think the fact that you come to church an hour a week qualifies you to tell me what needs to be done there?" Fortunately, I can honestly say that, 25 years later, that man is one of my dearest friends in the world. He was healthy enough to know that, although he had an opinion, it might or might not be adequately informed. May his tribe increase. Everyone seems to think that the care of bodies should be left to the professionals, but everyone is an expert in the care of that which is eternal.

This is not to say that church leadership must be delegated to the professionals, but it is a call to recognize that, as with all the rest of life, church has become increasingly complex, dynamic, and multi-faceted. When we treat its management and leadership as though anyone has the skills to do it, then we have decided to keep it irrelevant and unimportant. If our churches are to grow and change, to become relevant and transformational, the leadership must understand the impact of our *whitewater world* on our faith communities. Leading and managing a church's decline is something anyone can do. Leading a dynamic, vital, relevant and growing church is not. Why is the church the one institution that we believe can be adequately and successfully led by people who have no experience, expertise, training? How long would stockholders allow the management of a company to continue if that corporation had declined as consistently as the mainline church has? This is not a call to hierarchical leadership by church professionals; rather, it is a plea that we stop treating the church as so unimportant or so simplistic that anyone can lead it. At the very least, we need to recognize that having everyone vote on every issue, or simply electing a warm body and good soul, is not building the church of Jesus Christ in a healthy way.

Once upon a time people had work, family, and church and were deeply and personally invested in all three. Their full engagement gave them wisdom, insight, and expertise. The folks who have that level of engagement in our churches today must be retired, have little else to do with their lives, or have an overwhelming need to be in control. Like every other institution, the church is changing (or dying) so rapidly that even fulltime professionals cannot keep up with trends, innovations, and evolutions. Rare is the pastor or lay leader who can:

- Understand the sociological dynamics of how sites like Facebook have changed the way people communicate and connect.
- Design marketing programs that reach their community or congregation using social networking media.
- Create worship experiences that move at the rate of "The Avengers" rather than "Bonanza."
- Conceptualize year-round stewardship programs for people who no longer carry cash or checks.

- Lead a community that is becoming diverse, inclusive, and multicultural but with divergent needs and expectations.
- Empower spiritual formation within a community that is less and less informed about the Christian faith and more and more antagonistic to the institution of the church.
- Comprehend why data management is the highest value for successful and growing organizations and companies and how that applies to the church.
- Provide community, connection, and care for people who are likely to be commuting great distances just for worship.

This list could go on and on, but we clearly live in a world in which no one is able to have the kind of diverse expertise that is needed to be a comprehensively effective leader. To assume that an entire congregation can be adequately informed and even gather frequently enough to make visionary decisions is delusional.

The irony is that the complexity of our *whitewater world* is a powerful argument for a new form of leadership that involves the comprehensive wisdom and expertise of a congregation. This 21st-century form of congregationalism calls on each member to contribute to the body's collective wisdom. It does not assume that everyone is equally wise, insightful, and capable about everything. In this system, the pastor's (or pastors') principal role is to identify, recruit, and facilitate the community's shared expertise and wisdom. For example, rather than ask those gathered at a congregational meeting to decide the communication/marketing strategy for the coming year, the pastor should gather those in the community (members and not) who have expertise in this area. This is an area that is highly dynamic and changes almost daily. The pastor's role is to find resources to help these largely secular experts apply their wisdom to the unique needs of a church. Another role of the pastor is to help this newly convened group of congregational experts to understand the vision, mission, and strategic goals established by the congregation as a whole. These larger decisions guide and inform all other decisions.

Neither the pastor nor the council/board/consistory has the needed expertise to create, manage, or modify a 21st-century strategic and effective communication strategy. Because the congregation also does not have the skill, their role is to provide the larger context for the plan and, in many cases, ultimately to approve funding for the plan. That is the point at which real power is exercised. The council's role is to hold those implementing the plan accountable to their own goals by managing the monthly expenditure of funds. The role of the pastor and staff is to recruit, train, and coach this team of experts and ensure that their work is congruent with the vision the congregation holds. Essentially, congregational governance must come to mean the congregation sets the agenda for the church, but then empowers teams of experts to implement and execute that agenda.

Gil Rendle, in his book *Journey in the Wilderness*, argues persuasively that there are six norms the mainline church and its people must release in order to move ahead effectively in the 21st-century mission field.[4] Leadership coach and author Bill Easum would call these some of our most "sacred cows." Regardless of the quality of the gourmet burgers they might make, killing off these cows will require great courage, which, in my opinion, comes only from fully recognizing the desperation of our situation.[5] These are the norms Rendle suggests we must relinquish, followed by some of my thoughts:

The Assumption of Egalitarianism: The Tyranny of the All

Egalitarianism is often presented as the opposite of hierarchical leadership. One is good/holy while the other is bad/evil. This is a major tenet and core value for many progressive people of faith in the structure of organizations. The challenge in an egalitarian system, as Rendle effectively points out, is, in such a system, all needs, ideas, and voices are given equal weight and importance. This completely neglects the principle articulated most clearly by Vilfredo Pareto. The Pareto

---

[4] Gil Rendle, *Journey Into the Wilderness: New Life for Mainline Churches*, (Nashville: Abingdon Press, 2010), ch. 6

[5] Bill Easum, *Sacred Cows Make Gourmet Burgers: Ministry Anytime, Anywhere, By Anyone*, (Nashville: Abingdon Press, 1995)

Principle[6] is the recognition that 80 percent of our impact will come from 20 percent of our efforts. Therefore, rather than continuing to invest in the 80 percent that is not productive, we should target the places in which we can have the most impact.

In a setting with diminishing resources, we must acknowledge that wisdom and good stewardship require that we invest where there is the greatest possibility for the desired and needed results. The greatest change in a system will come by investing in those embracing change, but we spend too much of our energy on those who resist. Rendle says:

The practice of egalitarianism in which all must be treated equally and no one moves ahead until all are on board directs missional resources and attention toward weakness rather than strength ... egalitarianism requires leaders to focus 80 percent of their time, attention, and resources on the 20 percent of the system that demonstrates recalcitrance, weakness, inability, and disinterest.[7]

This does NOT advocate for a hierarchical approach to structure and leadership; however, it is a call to acknowledge that holding on to the old way of waiting to move ahead until all are ready to take the trip will cause us to miss the boat on this rapidly changing whitewater sea. In many settings, the value of congregationalism has been an excuse for inaction, and the need for total congregational buy-in has delayed decision-making so long as to make it ineffective or irrelevant. Too often, in the time required to ensure that everyone is ready and able to make a fully-informed decision, the target has moved, changed, or no longer matters.

The Assumption of Representative Democracy

Slaying this sacred cow may require even greater courage. The trouble with the idea of representative democracy is that it encourages people to represent the interest of one stakeholder or constituency sometimes to the

[6] Richard Koch, *The 80/20 Principle: The Secret to Achieving More with Less*, (New York: Doubleday, 2008) ch.1

[7] Rendle, *Journey Into the Wilderness*, ch. 6

detriment of the good of the entire body. To see the danger and destructiveness of this idea, look no further than the gridlock of the United States Congress under Donald Trump. In an increasingly partisan age, elected representatives seem utterly incapable of acting on behalf of the greater good for the entire nation. Indeed, their fear is based on the very real idea that their constituency will punish them if they serve any interest other than their own.

In a church, the role of leadership must be to call the entire organization to behave in the most strategic way to accomplish the congregation's stated goal. When a congregation votes to adopt or modify its vision, mission, or strategic goals it is giving the leadership their marching orders. Represented constituencies, projects, programs, and ministries then must align with the agenda the congregation has set. Anything else violates the congregational mandate. Vision, mission, and strategic goals must become the stars by which effective leaders navigate through everchanging and tumultuous seas. Remember: the shallower the water the greater the chance for whitewater and rapid change. Imagine a team in a raft shooting down the rapids. Decisions must be made on training, strategy, and mutual benefit. There is not time for six committees to meet and then call a congregational meeting. The church no longer is drifting slowly along on a lazy river singing "Kumbaya." We either will learn to navigate the whitewater or be swept away.

The old maps no longer work when the rate of change is this great, but, if we stay fixed on the stars rather than reacting to the changing scenery, an organization can make effective decisions and respond with great flexibility. This is the one area in which a congregation exercises absolute power. Members do not have the time or expertise to make daily, or even quarterly, decisions effectively. They must select leaders who will make those decisions and trust that they will be made based on what the congregation has said is their perception of who God has called them to be and where God has called them to go.

As Rendle points out, "The dilemma is that representational groups tend to be decisionphobic."[8] Every decision is ultimately a choice between one group or another, one good or another, one value or another.

---

[8] Rendle, *Journey Into the Wilderness*, ch. 6

As a result, decision-phobic leadership meetings revert to "a reporting agenda." That is, meetings consist of hearing reports rather than grappling with strategies for fulfilling the vision/mission/strategy the congregation has assigned. The other consequence of decision-phobic leadership is that they focus on problem solving. Solving problems makes a body feel justified in their work, and, hence, it almost always crowds out the more challenging strategic work.

For this reason, Rendle recommends a smaller board that represents the entire congregation and whose agenda is set by the larger decisions of the congregation. They listen widely and closely to the external mission field to which they have been assigned, not just to the competing constituents. In a healthy church the mission is externally focused, yet, without great diligence, the agenda of almost every leadership meeting will revert to internal needs and challenges. While those must be addressed, leaders need to resist letting that take over the agenda. The congregation, which elected the leadership, has set their agenda, and it hopefully is an external one. If the organization is a club the agenda is to serve the membership. If the organization is a church the agenda is to become the Body of Christ and to serve those whom Jesus served. True congregationalism allows the congregation to decide how they live out that calling, and it is rarely an agenda of self-service.

The Assumption of Scarcity

While most churches and denominations are being forced to try to do more with less, the choice is whether this is immobilizing or an opportunity to focus on the vital. Although there are "fixed" expenses and activities that consume most of our discretionary resources, the danger is when decisions are made based on fear and lack. One congregation said they would sell their 200-year-old building rather than allow it to decide its mission and ministry. That decision freed them to make creative decisions and to use the building as an asset rather than seeing it as a liability to be maintained or a museum to be preserved.

To allow a sense of lack, need, and scarcity to shape our decisions is to ensure that we are living out of a place of fear rather than faith. This is true for congregations that live week to week as well as for congregations who have huge endowments that they protect while letting the mission deteriorate. Fear deprives us of energy and ingenuity, and leadership then invests their time and energy in survival. This neglects the call of Jesus to be as a seed willing to fall to the ground and die. It ignores Paul's assertion that "if we live, we live to the Lord, and if we die, we die to the Lord; so then, whether we live or whether we die, we are the Lord's."[9]

The church does not belong to us, and, like every living body, there may come a time to die. None of the churches the Apostle Paul planted are still around. Making peace with our mortality is the only path to being free to live while we still are here. Life is the responsibility of the leadership and governance, not preservation. We are not called to be morticians preserving a dead Body of Christ.

The Assumption of Control

Rendle rightly suggests we must understand the difference between leadership and control. We expect leaders to be able to solve our problems and control our circumstances. Often, though, what really is needed to enable an organization to change and adapt to the contemporary age is not control but chaos.

In an earlier chapter, Rendle suggests that "the distinction between management and leadership ... has been used to make the point that management offers satisfaction to the system and leadership introduces discontent."[10] For change to be birthed, both pain and possibility must be present. The adaptive leadership needed in the 21st century is not tidy. God creates out of chaos. This is the witness of Genesis 1 and Acts 2. The illustration that we often use is that birth is a painful, noisy, messy, surprising process. Death is neat and orderly, quiet and sterile. Which outcome are we seeking?

Leadership manages the hopes and fears of a congregation. We must allow the fear to become great enough to motivate change and move us out of our stagnation and comfort. The danger, of course, is that the fear becomes too great and people freeze up or flee. The key is to offer

---

[9] Rom. 14:8, NRSV

[10] Rendle, *Journey in the Wilderness*, ch. 5

sufficient hope so people are motivated to move toward a preferable future. Creating a culture of both push and pull is leadership, not resolving everyone's problems and presenting it in a neat pill to be swallowed.

Rather than giving answers to the challenging questions, effective leaders remove the constraints to free and open conversation in the hope that new solutions may emerge. Also, if a ready-made solution is offered it inevitably will meet resistance, but a solution that emerges from a conversation in which many voices have been heard is much more likely to have a chance to succeed in achieving the changes that are vital.

Calvin Pava of the Harvard Business School talks about "disorderly planning."[11] In previous ages, linear or incremental approaches might have been effective, but, today, leaders must embrace and, if necessary, create disorder/chaos. In highly complex or conflicted situations, leaders must resist the temptation to exercise authority and, instead, abide in the midst of the chaos as a non-anxious presence. Helping a community live into the pain and possibility of a situation greatly enhances the quality of the outcome and the likelihood of systemic change. Disorderly planning "does not seek to require uniformity and does not move neatly ahead. Rather, leadership identifies a measurable or describable goal or outline. It is not neat or comfortable and requires learning not just new skills, but new ways of being in the world." Asking leaders to help us move into ill-defined and complex new problems cannot live if we continue to impose the old standard rewards for control, neatness, and uniformity of a managerial time and a managerial church.

The image that comes to mind is from Deuteronomy when God is described as behaving like a mother eagle. When the time is right, she removes the soft padding from the nest, making it an uncomfortable place to be. Then she begins to remove some of the branches, which destabilizes the setting. Finally, she hovers over the nest, flapping her great wings, forcing her young into the air where, despite the terror of falling, they learn to use their wings and fly. Currently, too much of church structure and leadership is designed for comfort and security, and our

---

[11] Calvin Pava, "New Strategies of Systems Change: Reclaiming Nonsynoptic Methods," http://journals.sagepub.com/doi/abs/10.1177/001872678603900702, (July 1, 1986)

congregations never discover that they were made to soar on the Winds of the Spirit. The choice is ours: the nest or the winds?

The Assumption of Harmony

Rendle cites a "favorite observation" from author Wally Armbruster. "If everybody's singing the same note that ain't harmony. That, baby, is monotony. Harmony happens when people sing different notes."[12] Harmony is birthed out of dissonance, NOT uniformity. In one church I worked with the leader dominated every meeting, but, in her mind, things were productive and harmonious. My observation was the leadership had used race and gender to intimidate or coerce everyone into compliance, and very little of significance was accomplished in those meetings. In any relationship, if two people always come to the same conclusion then one of them is redundant.

Healthy conflict according to Rendle is nothing more than two or more ideas occupying the same space at the same time. While conflict in the church often reaches unhealthy or destructive levels, differing views, opinions, and goals are critical for the church to move forward and out of stagnation and decline. The absence of these life-giving tensions is the sign that what we are building is not what M. Scott Peck labeled "pseudocommunity."[13]

In pseudocommunities, leadership identifies the options, says, "I suggest ..." and then moves to a vote. This compulsion to vote on everything and to treat a vote as an outcome often avoids real issues and opportunities. Living with the chaos a bit, encouraging the expression of counterviews, and turning a situation over and over just might result in a better decision. The community that is birthed certainly will be more genuine. Voting is a win/lose proposition. The majority rules. The minority loses, even though they may be right. A better model might be to listen to one another and then seek to listen authentically to the Spirit.

---

[12] Rendle, *Journey in the Wilderness*, ch. 5

[13] M. Scott Peck, *The Different Drum: Community Making and Peace*, (New York: Touchstone, 1987), 86

Change is almost always the outcome that is needed, and it is more likely to emerge from a sacred conversation than from a right vote. Whenever possible, consensus must be allowed to grow, and when it is achieved a vote is sacrilegious. Consensus grows out of conversation in which differing voices are heard and honored, and the entire group seeks the Voice of Wisdom (Sophia) before reaching an agreed strategy for moving forward. This is hard work, and it is often messy. Unlike the artificial harmony that many churches seem to value, however, the community that emerges is stronger, healthier, and more diverse. Voting and majority rule may be the "American way," but they are not always the Way of Jesus.

The Assumption that Ministry Can't be Measured

In systems that are faced with ongoing decline the trend is to denigrate the typical ways in which success, growth, and vitality are measured. It is an important corrective to hear that we need to go beyond, what Reggie McNeal in his book *Missional Renaissance* calls, "the scorecard" of "how many, how often, how much."[14] Jesus changed the world with a congregation of twelve. The key word in that sentence, though, is not "twelve," but "changed."

The true measure of a church must be determined by its impact on the community. The danger with that is how it is measured. The Bible models measuring. Look at how often we are told specific numbers. The interesting thing in the New Testament, though, is we are never told the number of satisfied community members sitting in the pews on Sunday. Rather, we are told how many people were converted, baptized, healed, or fed. They measured their impact, not their size. Of course, the community of faith grew, but not because growth was their objective. If happiness is the byproduct of a life well lived, growth is the outcome of a church that lives out of a powerful vision and a compelling mission.

Rendle writes, "Regarding measures, a system gets what it pays attention to. Another way to say the same thing is that a system produces

[14] Reggie McNeal, *Missional Renaissance: Changing the Scorecard for the Church*, (San Francisco: Jossey-Bass, 2009), xvii

what it measures. If the system measures nothing that is what it gets. Without measures we cannot focus on what we are called to produce."[15]

Measuring means that we must let go of our fear and then fearlessly reexamine what we do and why. We must ask if it is working and if it is carrying us toward our vision and fulfilling our mission, and if it is the best strategy for becoming who God has called us to be and what God has asked us to do.

Congregationalism too often has meant little more than the congregation voting on anything and everything. The practical result has been the same small group of over-invested people making the same types of decisions that they made, or that their parents made, 50 years ago. The rapid death of the mainline church seems an incidental factor in their decision making, as does the reality of radical and relentless change. Church governance is the most classic example of sticking our heads in the sand that exists in modern society. We keep acting as if nothing has changed and ignoring all contrary evidence that we might need to find new ways of doing things.

So, what does effective 21st-century congregationalism look like?

The church is led but not managed by the congregation. The congregation makes the really large decisions that determine all other decisions: What is our vision? What is our mission? Who are our leaders? How will we spend our resources? Once those decisions are made, the staff and elective leadership must become experts in discovering how to do what the congregation has said must be done.

The congregation selects, empowers, and holds accountable leaders, not managers. The leaders may need to select managers, but the congregation needs leaders who can take a 30,000-foot view of the world, the community, and the church. Living in a whitewater world, the church cannot afford to meet frequently enough to make constant course corrections but, instead, needs leaders who can make them according to the direction the congregation has determined. Monthly leadership meetings focus on vision, not reports that can be read at home.

The congregation gives leaders permission to fail. In fact, the congregation should require them to fail regularly, and one failure a year

---

[15] Rendle, *Journey in the Wilderness*, ch. 5

must be significant. Imagine a congregational meeting at which the pastor and other staff members must report their failures rather than their successes. In a culture in which failure is fatal no faith will ever be exercised. Leaders will become managers who take the safest course, which, generally, is to stay in the nest regardless of how uncomfortable it is or how the muscles in our wings atrophy. If the congregation can create an atmosphere in which failures are expected, then change can happen. Michael Jordan said, "I missed over 9,000 shots. I failed over and over, which is why I succeeded." Although incompetency should not be encouraged, a willingness to try new things must be.

Resource the outcomes the congregation desires. If making it safely to death with plenty of money in the bank is the church's vision, then it needs to act accordingly. If, however, the vision involves transforming the community to which God has sent the church then the budget and staff should be aligned with an external focus. If we are a club, we hire people and spend money primarily to make our lives more comfortable. If we are the Body of Christ, then the budget the church adopts and the goals the congregation sets should be geared toward those who are the real "customers." It has been said that our checkbook (back when we used them) and our calendars tell the truth about us. If we are spending all our resources on ourselves and our own, then we already have been judged and found wanting by a hurting humanity. The staff will serve those who pay them, unless the congregation continuously redirects their efforts outward.

In an authentic and effective congregational system, the members really are the ministers of the church. They care less and less about voting and more and more about serving. They exercise their power by taking back the ministry of the church from the hired help. The Bible says that the function of the pastor is "to equip the saints for the work of ministry."[16] We gather on Sundays to be nourished, and then we scatter to serve. A church is truly congregational when all its members are mobilized for ministry rather than management. Such a church is highly attractive to the unchurched and young people who want their lives to make a difference and have learned already that little of life-changing

---

[16] Eph. 4:12, NRSV

consequence is accomplished in meetings. Perhaps the church should pass a rule that, other than worship, we must stand up for meetings and we can sit down only if what we are doing is ministry. Effective congregationalism meets once a year to consider only the issues that will govern all other issues: vision, mission, strategy, and leadership. After that the only decisions that are made by anyone are expressions of the will of the congregation that has been expressed clearly and repeatedly.

It is said that the definition of crazy is doing the same thing over and over and expecting different results. The result of governing a church using 200-year-old systems and structures has been decline and death. Perhaps it is time to open the windows and let the Spirit blow through. It might make a mess, but remember that Creation and the church are proof that God works best in chaos. What we are doing clearly isn't working because we are dying. What's the worst that can happen if we try something new? Perhaps we will fall into the hands of a graceful God, or maybe we will learn to soar again.

WORSHIP WITH A CAPITAL "W"

T hat is how a reporter once described worship at the Cathedral of Hope.[1] Worship became the number one reason people visited Virginia-Highland Church. Although this is changing in many places, worship is the front door for the overwhelming majority of churches in America. In other words, worship is the reason people visit a church and then choose to visit again. Conversely, it also can be the backdoor of a church, or the number one reason people visit but do not return or join. The decline of mainline churches is probably a substantial critique about what most of us are doing on Sunday mornings.

It is tempting to conclude that vital worship is about style or theology. Marjorie H. Royle, who has written extensively about worship, congregational vitality, and clergy leadership, writes:

All in all, quality worship experience is important for congregations that want to grow. Because our culture is changing, congregations may need to change and innovate in their worship to create such an experience. However, faith tradition is important. Drums and projection screens [forms of contemporary worship] do not fit in every tradition or with every age group. Innovation and change need to occur within a congregation's faith tradition. Finding the balance between the two is one of the major challenges of worship in the 21st Century.[2]

Royle says, "Congregations that have adopted innovative worship and contemporary worship styles are significantly more likely to have grown

[1] George Exoo, "GOD'S Country," *D Magazine*, https://www.dmagazine.com/publications/d-magazine/1997/september/gods-country/, (September 1997)
[2] Marjorie H. Royle, "Facts on Worship 2010," http://faithcommunitiestoday.org/sites/default/files/FACTs-on-Worship.pdf, 14

in the last five years, a new report has found. Contemporary worship seems particularly important in attracting young adults."[3]

Worship at the Cathedral of Hope (a megachurch) and Virginia-Highland Church can be classified as traditional or liturgical in that the clergy wear vestments, there is a robed choir, hymns are sung, the liturgical calendar and lectionary are followed, and the Eucharist is served at every service. Many of those in attendance, however, consider the worship "contemporary" because multimedia is used, and each service includes contemporary spiritual lessons from the common culture alongside traditional scriptural lessons. A colleague labeled this style of worship "enlivened vintage worship."

Purists might assess this kind of worship as conflicted or even contradictory in style, but it has successfully created congregations that are substantially younger than most mainline churches. This may be due in part to a phenomenon that late columnist and bestselling author Rachel Held Evans described in an oft-quoted article in the "Washington Post." She posits that:

Recent research from Barna Group and the Cornerstone Knowledge Network found that 67 percent of millennials prefer a "classic" church over a "trendy" one, and 77 percent would choose a "sanctuary" over an "auditorium." While we have yet to warm to the word "traditional" (only 40 percent favor it over "modern"), millennials exhibit an increasing aversion to exclusive, closed-minded religious communities masquerading as the hip new places in town. For a generation bombarded with advertising and sales pitches, and for whom the charge of "inauthentic" is as cutting an insult as any, church rebranding efforts can actually backfire, especially when young people sense that there is more emphasis on marketing Jesus than actually following Him. Millennials "are not disillusioned with tradition; they are frustrated with slick or shallow expressions of religion," argues David Kinnaman, who interviewed hundreds of them for Barna Group

---

[3] Ibid. 1

and compiled his research in "You Lost Me: Why Young Christians Are Leaving Church ... and Rethinking Faith."[4]

The late theologian Robert Webber coined the phrase "ancient-future worship."[5] In his book *Evangelicals on the Canterbury Trail: Why Evangelicals Are Attracted to the Liturgical Church*, Webber recounts his own journey and that of six others who sought to recover from what he called "historical amnesia."[6] Since the book was published in 1985, when Rachel Held Evans was four years old, Webber was prescient about what millennials might find attractive in mainline churches. Given the witness of these two very different lovers of the church, we might logically ask, "If their conclusions are true, why then are most mainline sanctuaries largely empty on Sunday mornings?"

Although my experience with enlivened vintage worship has been positive, it is not my conclusion that this is the formula for church growth. There are, however, some underlying principles that might strengthen worship, regardless of the style, and make it more attractive to a new generation of churchgoers.

Assume nothing.

My two daughters are classic millennials in many ways. One of them observed that her peers don't dislike the church, but they don't really know anything about it. She talked about how her friends were fascinated that she was a "preacher's kid," and were filled with all kinds of questions.

---

[4] Rachel Held Evans, "Want millennials back in the pews? Stop trying to make church 'cool.'." https://www.washingtonpost.com/opinions/jesus-doesnt-tweet/2015/04/30/fb07ef1a-ed01-11e4-8666-a1d756d0218e_story.html?utm_term=.f95bb60cecaa (April 30. 2015)

[5] Drew Dyck, "Explainer: Ancient-Future Worship," *Christianity Today*, http://www.christianitytoday.com/pastors/2009/may-online-only/explainer-ancient-future-worship.html

[6] Robert Webber and Lester Ruth, *Evangelicals on the Canterbury Trail: Why Evangelicals Are Attracted to the Liturgical Church* (New York: Morehouse Publishing, 1985)

My children, literally, were among the first to grow up in the Cathedral of Hope. The church became a part of the United Church of Christ in 2003, so was never a part of the predecessor denominations, meaning it joined a relatively new denomination that still is learning to live out the values it espouses nationally. The Cathedral, therefore, had to teach every new member what it meant to be a part of that community and their denomination.

In terms of worship, the UCC afforded great freedom because the church was not bound by the traditions of the historically Congregational Church nor the Evangelical and Reformed Church. As one of the few pure UCC churches, the Cathedral of Hope felt free to design worship in the most meaningful way for them. Almost all Protestant churches technically share this freedom but are hidebound by traditions and expectations. Because they were inventing their own worship tradition, CoH found it incumbent that they explain everything they did in worship each time there was a change. They also adopted a value of changing worship with each liturgical season so that no practice became too engrained, thus they were able to celebrate in a more ecumenical way.

In explaining why things were done as they were, the leadership discovered that the experience of those who had been worshipping their entire lives was enriched because they finally understood what each element meant, where it came from, and why it was valuable and important. If it wasn't possible to explain, then it didn't need to be done. New people felt less excluded because they learned something new, and they valued the experience from the start.

Socrates, in his trial for impiety, famously espoused, "The unexamined life is not worth living." That reality also might be applied to worship. If we do not understand, value, and appreciate what we do, say, or sing well enough to explain it to the faithful and convince the seeking, then perhaps we should stop. Perhaps nothing contributes more to moribund worship than doing things simply because that is what always has been done. Millennials value ritual and traditions, but not for their own sake. It might be a mystical or even metaphysical experience; that is the point. There should be a point to all of worship, so **assume nothing**.

It is all about energy.

Worship should be passionate, and it should impassion people, infusing them with devotion and facilitating the expression of that devotion.

This doesn't make Pentecostal worship superior to contemplative compline services, it simply speaks to the fact that, although the energy may be different in each of these settings, it is equally important in both. There is, of course, an old solution to boring sermons: wake up the preacher. The same can be said of all liturgical elements.

In a concert I attended, the musician apologized for the nonsensical lyrics of the song he was about to perform. He needn't have bothered because it was an old and beloved tune that soon had the entire audience on their feet clapping, swaying, and singing along. It left me wondering why this happens so seldom in church. Perhaps it is because those charged with designing worship are so obsessed with the lyrics of worship that they forget to focus on the tune, the beat, the rhythm, and the power of the experience.

It is truer than ever that people do not need church, worship, or the preacher to teach them about God. Most congregants have access to more information in their pocket than they ever could assimilate about any topic that stirs their curiosity. They don't need to know about God; they need to know God. Effective worship, regardless of the style, should afford the worshipper an opportunity to encounter the Divine/Holy/Sacred/Other. That will not happen intellectually; if it did, everyone with a PhD would be a saint.

Historically-black churches understand this much better than dry, intellectual, left-brained, white mainline churches. The well-educated clergy of the mainline once served the community well, but, these days, that education can lead to the very hubris that turns off those who come seeking an experience they cannot find in a classroom or club, nor from a charity. Even native New Englanders, not known for their enthusiasm, have the capacity to express fervor at concerts or sporting events. Why are our churches so devoid of this quality of energy? Is it racism that causes us to avoid the expressions of passion found in many historically-black churches? Perhaps it is classism that makes us fearful to raise our hands, clap, rise to our feet, sing along, sway, and weep.

The Cathedral of Hope built a worship facility that seats approximately 1,000, but, at the church's peak, the building still proved inadequate for Easter and Christmas Eve. So, we rented the symphony center, which seats 2,200, and filled it twice on each holy day. That was an extraordinary experience, but the local gay men's chorus, the Turtle Creek Chorale, filled the same space half-a-dozen times for their Christmas concert. These concerts were attended by a remarkably diverse cross-section of the community. This was most impressive considering it was Texas. In a conversation with then-Artistic Director Dr. Tim Seelig, I asked if he thought he really was the best choral conductor, or if there was another explanation for their extraordinary success. Tim demurred at my compliment and said, "It isn't about the music, or at least that isn't the only reason for our success." He went on to explain that, in addition to well-prepared, diverse, beautiful music, he made sure that, in every concert, those who attended laughed, cried, and got chill-bumps.

Although worship must avoid being emotionally manipulative, it must not be void of emotion. We are commanded to love God with our whole being—heart, soul, mind, and strength. Mainline worship is very good with the mind component, but, to paraphrase Jesus quoting Deuteronomy, "Man (and woman) shall not live by head alone." Worship should stir our hearts and move our souls at least as much as it helps us make up our mind about who we are called by God to be.

True worship requires a response.

Loving God with our "strength" means gathering with sisters and brothers to love and adore God regularly and then scattering to be the people of God. Effective worship should inspire, energize, nourish, and transform people, then set them loose on an unsuspecting world to be the risen Body of Christ.

We were taught in seminary that sermons should tell people not just "what" but also "so what." Worship too often does not lead the people of God to express their faith through words and deeds that transform the world. At other times, though, progressive churches gather on Sunday and spend most of the time with announcements, and then listening to sermons, prayers, and liturgy decrying the problems of the world, but never get around to making love to the One who called us together. What distinguishes an effective church from an effective social justice organization is our connection and regular reconnection to the source of Light/Life/Love.

Making that connection and subsequent expression explicit is vital. Millennials want to invest their time, money, and energy in making a difference. There are thousands of places where they can do that. The church is unique because spending our lives making an impact for good is an expression of our faith and our love affair with the God of all people and all creation. It is holy work sustained by the holy food of entering "God's presence with thanksgiving and God's courts with praise."[7]

There is nothing new or revolutionary about gathering to worship/scattering to serve, but most churches seem to have neglected one side or the other. Worship should be crafted in such a way that it transforms the worshipping community into the Body of Christ. It should be deliberate about offering transformational moments for the heart and soul, not just the mind. Only then can we scatter to love God with all our strength.

Worship with a capital "W" is done well.

Regardless of the style, worship with a capital "W" requires a significant investment of time to plan, review, and anticipate. Nothing takes more planning than spontaneity. Some preachers insist that they don't need to prepare a sermon because God will give them what to say. This ultimately proves to be an excuse to blame God for our own laziness and lack of preparation. God does inspire great sermons, yes, but the Spirit can be heard much more clearly when we have done our research and preparation and then given these tools to the Spirit so she can inspire us.

When I am most prepared I am most freely responsive to the Spirit and the congregation. There are times when circumstances of life rob me of the time to be as prepared as I'd like, and, fortunately, God seems to compensate for that. My theory, however, always has been that, if I will

---

[7] Psalm 100:4

do the best I can to do the work, God will make up the difference. So it is with worship.

Every single element of worship should be carefully chosen, thought through, rehearsed—at least in our minds—energetically led, and then ruthlessly reviewed. Small elements, like waiting while a worship leader gets up and walks to the lectern, create "dead air" that you would never see on TV or hear on radio. It is so common in worship, however, that few of us give it a second thought, but the subconscious message it sends is clear. Those who grew up in a culture devoid of "dead air" get the clear message that this is not important enough to be planned and prepared as well as what they see on television. When done well, a service flows seamlessly from one element to another. No one notices, but the impact is powerful. Unbroken energy can increase or decrease depending on what is needed. Dead air serves no purpose except to diminish the importance of what is about to be read or said or sung.

Dr. Marcia McFee is a renowned worship consultant, and her most powerful lesson is around the issue of how to pace worship. She warns that when the activities of a service are segmented by starts and stops a service seems to last forever because of how our mind experiences time. If, however, a service flows seamlessly from one element or one moment to another, rising and falling without notice or break, the service is done before you know it. She observes that most worship is "checking off a to-do list. First you do this and then you do this," and she calls it "flatlining."[8]

Crafting a well-designed, seamless experience of the Holy takes work, practice, and review. We need to be willing to walk through the previous service in excruciating detail and courageously acknowledge what worked well and what didn't. Continuous honest review and improvement are the only way to achieve worship with a capital "W" consistently.

---

[8] Marcia McFee, "Flatlining - Worship Vitality Killers," https://www.youtube.com/watch?v=CsvxeW-d9DQ

Great worship that attracts the next generation will have to be courageously inclusive.

Diversity is a lot like the weather: everyone talks about it, but few do much. Time and again, congregations that proclaim progressive and inclusive values look as homogenous as churches that are excluding or fundamentalist. Walking the walk is one of the most difficult challenges for many well-meaning congregations to meet. To be fair, there is a cost associated with becoming an authentically diverse community. Still, it is one of the highest values for millennials, and it is not optional. A report from the Brookings Institute found that, "Racial diversity will be the most defining and impactful characteristic of the millennial generation."[9]

Ironically, many churches seem less committed to inclusive language than they were 40 years ago. Although gender-inclusive language was once a core expectation in seminaries, those policies have been relaxed substantially. This is a frustration to many younger women and to men who care about justice issues and changing gender inequality. Theologian Mary Daly was correct when, decades ago, she first observed that, "If God is male then the male is God."[10] Most mainline churches seem incapable of changing human language, let alone divine language. So long as we sing about "mankind" or talk about "brotherhood," young women will find the church a place of oppression. Lesbian, gay, bisexual, and transgender (LGBT) and other queer people long have been oppressed by religions that deify the masculine and hold the feminine as inferior. Homophobia is the other side of the coin of sexism, so having a rainbow flag on your building while worshipping a purely masculine God is hypocrisy. This puts the lie to what we say about welcoming all people and all of every person. So long as only the masculine is holy the female part of every person is not truly welcomed on holy ground.

---

[9] William H. Frey, "Diversity defines the millennial generation," The Brookings Institution, https://www.brookings.edu/blog/the-avenue/2016/06/28/diversity-defines-the-millennial-generation/ (June 28, 2016)

[10] Mary Daly, *Beyond God the Father: Toward a Philosophy of Women's Liberation* (Boston: Beacon Press, 1985), 19

A great deal has been written about this, but confronting it may be the test of how serious we are about being a truly welcoming, diverse, and inclusive place. Is this really our highest value, or do we care more about the traditional words with which we are comfortable? In the end, the language we use may be less significant than the truth it tells about who we are despite the clichés on our websites. The same is true if the only music we sing is European or the only language spoken in our services is that of the ruling majority. What changes would your congregation embrace to become more fully diverse and welcoming?

When Virginia-Highland Church called me, they thought they were embracing their diversity because I was an openly gay man in a long-term gay relationship. They were quite proud that they were liberal enough to call the person who, for two decades, led the largest LGBT church in the world. In the midst of that self-congratulation, though, we discovered real resistance to changing the language of hymns, especially Christmas carols. The choir fought about this regularly, even though we routinely changed the language of scripture (things like "Son of Man" to "Human One"). It took considerable effort, courage, and deliberate persistence for them to acknowledge that gender-inclusive language is the only way to have integrity about what they claim to be their core values.

As a Southern white man, making worship more racially inclusive was a logistical challenge. There were few people of color (one) in the congregation when I arrived, so we had to be creative. Fortunately, the congregation still was at the point of knowing they had to make some significant changes if they were to survive when a donor bought two large, flat-screen televisions for the sanctuary. While there was significant resistance, everyone agreed to try this as an experiment that could be removed if the TVs distracted from worship or the aesthetics of the sanctuary. From that moment on, we worked very hard to ensure that images of Jesus, Mary, God, and others were almost always people of color. A new African-American family visited with their preteen son and teenaged daughter. Because of the diverse images on the screens, they stayed and became the cornerstones of that congregation's rebirth. The kids often served as liturgists, and, when I left, the mother was the president of the congregation.

While the church still is not as diverse as its city, it is far more diverse than the neighborhood in which it is located. On any given Sunday, attendance is four to five times what it was before we began using multimedia. The average age is 15 years younger than the median in the denomination's other congregations, and 20 years younger than I was when I was the senior pastor.[11] Fifty percent of the congregation currently is non-white or non-heterosexual. While this cannot be attributed fully to the use of multimedia, it did prove to be a powerful way to reinforce the church's values, and it allowed us to bring different voices, faces, images, and music into worship in ways that would have been otherwise impossible for a small congregation with few financial resources.

The screens compliment a service in which there are processions, vestments, the Eucharist, and traditional hymns. Millennials are able to reclaim ancient traditions in a setting that uses technology that they take for granted. Older people find it easier to see and even hear. When Miss Blanche, the church's matriarch, gave her blessings to the new screens because she could better read the words I knew technology and multimedia had arrived to stay. The total cost for the audio-visual system was around $10,000, but it paid for itself quickly with the families it attracted within weeks of its installation. Allowing a congregation in which the most visible face (the pastor's) was white and male to bring in female, Latin, African, and Asian faces and voices was powerfully effective in transforming the faces seated in the congregation. In a membership class held shortly before I left, there were two 50-plus-year-old women, four African-American women, two African-American youth, a heterosexual father, and a heterosexual millennial couple who were about to be married. The two deacons who presented the new members with their aprons, a gift symbolizing our belief that, as a member, you "take off your bib and put on your apron," both were gay men. A lay person remarked after the service that she believed that was what the "beloved community" was meant to look like.

---

[11] Michael Lipka, "Which U.S. religious groups are oldest and youngest?", Pew Research Center, http://www.pewresearch.org/fact-tank/2016/07/11/which-u-s-religious-groups-are-oldest-and-youngest/, (July 11, 2016)

A RUDDER FOR SAILING IN A SHALLOW SEA

H ardly a week passes in my consulting practice when I am not contacted by a congregation requesting resources or assistance to develop a strategic plan. We generally explain that, while it might be profitable for us, it would not be productive for them. In a 2014 article, "Forbes" declared strategic planning dead.[1] The "Stanford Social Innovation Review" agreed that the time of creating thick black binders with five-year plans had passed in an age of rapid adaptation and transformation. They wisely added, however, that nonprofits still need what they call a clear and compelling "adaptive strategy" for the future.[2]

President Dwight Eisenhower said, "Plans are useless, but planning is everything." Recognizing this makes it imperative that every congregation go through processes that clarify who they are and who they want to be, and what they do and what they should be doing, all based on a clear set of guiding values matched to an accurate awareness of community and world needs. Core values, vision, and mission are more crucial for vitality than ever before because one of the realities of shallow seas is that things can change very rapidly. For an institution that is as provincial as most churches, this global reality of living in a whitewater world can be quite disturbing. If we can learn to become agile and adaptive, however, the opportunities are tremendous.

It is a great irony that dying churches usually are well-managed. Thriving churches are chaotic because they are "permission-giving." In

---

[1] Bill Conerly, "The Death of Strategic Planning: Why?", Forbes magazine, https://www.forbes.com/forbes/welcome/?toURL=https://www.forbes.com/sites/billco nerly/2014/03/24/the-death-of-strategic-planning-why/&refURL, (March 24, 2014)

[2] Dana O'Donovan and Noah Rimland Flower, "The Strategic Plan is Dead. Long Live Strategy.", Stanford Social Innovation Review, https://ssir.org/articles/entry/the_strategic_plan_is_dead._long_live_strategy,_(January 10, 2013)

his book *Sacred Cows Make Gourmet Burgers*, Bill Easum talks about this as a critical principle. The great contrast between growing churches and dying ones can be understood by thinking about how a maternity ward compares to a mortuary.[3] Funeral homes are quiet, orderly, neat, and predictable. Everything stays exactly the way it is. Maternity wards are noisy, chaotic, unpredictable, and full of life. It might be good to remember that the creation parables of Genesis 1 and Acts 2 describe how the Spirit gives birth to the new out of chaos.

If a church has become so enmeshed with management, control, and administration that the strongest and best leaders are putting most of their time and energy here, this may be the first challenge that needs to be addressed. For God to reveal a new vision, a new mission, and a new day, churches must be willing to relinquish some control and, instead, exercise some faith.

For a church to give itself permission to be "born again," windows and doors must be opened so the Spirit might blow through like the wind. Jesus described the Spirit in just such language and reminded us that, "You do not know where the wind comes from or where it is going. That is how it is with anyone who is born of the Spirit."[4] That is how it must be for any church that would be reborn of the Spirit.

Relinquishing control and reducing regulation don't mean that the role of leaders is diminished. Leadership is influence. Management is control. This is a time when leaders, not managers, are needed. A prescribed process isn't really the critical piece of transformation. What is needed is ensuring that people are clear and committed to participating in the spiritual renewal of the church, as well as their own, by listening for a compelling new vision and then committing to a life-changing mission.

When the American birthrate was high churches could replenish their ranks with the children of members, or at least those who grew up in certain traditions. None of that is true anymore. Like any organization, business, or product, churches must attract new members, and that is dependent in large part on being clear about our values, vision, and

---

[3] Bill Easum, *Sacred Cows Make Gourmet Burgers: Ministry Anytime, Anywhere, By Anyone*, (Nashville: Abingdon Press, 1995)

[4] John 3:8

mission. Clarity of purpose is a cliché, but it is not sufficient that insiders alone gain this clarity. Effectively communicating it externally is vital to attract the next generation who likely did not grow up in your, or perhaps any, church.

We will examine new tools for effective communication in the next chapter, but what many, if not most, mainline churches struggle with is having something worth communicating. With churches declining in almost every town and neighborhood, what is it that makes your congregation worthy of surviving and thriving again? What makes it distinctive, compelling, and attractive to people who have little free time and want to invest it in ways that have impact? Few vintage churches can answer that with integrity, and that explains why so few younger members are attracted to them.

Once upon a time, youth grew up, went away to college, and dropped out of church ... until they had children, and then they returned. That is no longer the case. In fact, younger families with children now face the prospect of withholding athletics and other activities from their children because, increasingly, they are scheduled for Sunday mornings. Few churches are prepared to articulate in a compellingly way why participating in worship is of greater benefit to families and children than attending their daughter's soccer match or going with their son to a friend's Sunday morning birthday party.

Congregations that are wary of identifying and articulating their core values find they are trying to brand and market mush. No one is attracted to a church that cannot express who they are and how they are distinct. The most valued currency in life is time, and churches must compete for it along with everyone else. It may be a good thing that we are forced to reexamine just why people should choose to invest their time with us rather than outdoors with the kids getting exercise. If we can't make our own case, then perhaps we should cease to function and give our facilities to others who are impacting lives and the community.

Having gone through a process to identify the congregation's common core values, the vision of what the community believes they are called to become, and how that should be uniquely lived out in mission, a church is ready to develop a strategy. It should be agile and adaptable because the world is constantly changing. Every year, and sometimes every month, a congregation must be willing to reconsider the **HOW** by which they pursue the **WHY** of their existence. Vision, mission, and values become the stars by which a church navigates through a whitewater world. These guiding points allow for quicker decisions and greater responsiveness.

Freed from being guided by traditions and bylaws, churches that navigate by the stars of values, vision, and mission are able to experiment with new programs and ministries, so long as they are congruent with those three clear guiding principles. This allows for a more permission-giving attitude that encourages members to become ministers who are willing to try new things. The church must become an incubator for these ministry experiments because that is the only way to discover what will and won't work in the midst of such dramatic cultural changes. This "ready-fire-aim" approach to ministry invites a shift from members being consumers of church to them understanding that they are the church.

Let me offer two examples of how this principle found expression in the Virginia-Highland Church.

After an 18-month process, in which more than 80 percent of the congregation participated, the church unanimously adopted a vision that is succinctly expressed in Micah 6:8:

God has shown you O mortal what is good, and what does our God require of you but to do justice, love mercifully, and walk humbly with your God.

"Do. Love. Walk." became the hallmark of that congregation. Loving mercifully found primary expression in the church's extensive homeless ministry. That was coupled with doing justice, which meant working with the city and state to address issues that cause homelessness in one of the nation's wealthiest cities. They believe mercy and justice to be two sides of the same coin, and both are expressions of walking humbly with God. Worship and spiritual formation for adults, youth, and children became focused on empowering and nourishing a passion in people for justice and mercy.

We created new branding, creeds, music, studies, and more to continuously reinforce these ideas until every single member of the church will be able to articulate the mission and vision of the church. As a result, someone once approached a member with a proposition that we start a preschool in the extensive education space we have that sits empty much of the week. The member asked who the preschool might serve, and, when she learned that the intent was to serve the neighborhood, she informed the person that it was highly unlikely that the church would find that acceptable. You see, the neighborhood where the church is located is quite affluent, and many of the children would be dropped off by nannies and maids. She explained that, if what they had in mind was a preschool that served low-income families or that cared for the children of the poor or homeless, that would receive overwhelming support. This member did refer the matter to the governing body, but they agreed with her completely.

On the other hand, what has become the hallmark ministry of the church was started by a lay member asking a member of the staff if she thought the church would be willing to support the homeless ministry he had started. Originally, it was little more than offering water to those who lived outside during hot Atlanta summers. The staff member asked what was needed, and, realizing that all the member really wanted was to ask others to help, she approved the request and offered to be his first volunteer. This million-dollar ministry was begun without anyone voting to approve it. A lay minster in the church simply wanted to express his walk with God by loving mercifully and doing justice. The congregation already had voted on the vision/mission, and, because it didn't have budget impact, the ministry didn't require anyone else's vote. The timing was critical, and it was able to begin quickly in response to what was an immediate need. In most churches, by the time it could have been vetted and approved, summer would have turned to winter and blankets would have been needed rather than water and several of our friends who live outside would have been taken to the hospital for dehydration.

What began as a small experiment by a single member/minister attracted the participation of a significant portion of the congregation and was able to expand organically. It never cost the church money but attracted the attention of a donor in Texas who sent a check for $250,000. They subsequently have given $1 million because of the efficiency and effectiveness of this ministry. The church not only serves the homeless, but it has had significant impact on the city of Atlanta, which approved a $25 million bond package to house Atlanta's homeless population. What once was one of the worst cities on this issue now is well on its way to being a national leader. In part, this is happening because one person took the church's vision and mission seriously, and the church empowered them rather than seeking to control them.

Sailing in a whitewater/turbulent sea means you no longer can navigate by fixed points along the established shore. We must push into the deep where the water is constantly shifting and changing. In the midst of such turbulence, books of bylaws are non-productive cargo weighing down our common vessel. To be sure, there should be the necessary rules about finances, personnel, and the safety of children, but, beyond that, the church must find principles that are flexible and adaptable for the changing world in which we sail.

To reiterate:

- Having a clear and compelling vision/mission is the way congregationalism governs a 21st century church.
- Having clarity of core values provides the distinctiveness needed for decision making.
- Having a joyful freedom to experiment AND frequently fail opens the window for the Spirit to blow through and enhance the discovery of new ways to be the church today.

At some point, we must trust God again. That is the "walking humbly" part. Yes, some of the things we try will fail, but if we do not make failure something to fear we will learn and grow and find new ministries that work to fulfil the church's mission and make God's vision for us come to pass. A "ready-fire-aim" approach means that you *ready* yourself by doing adequate preparation in the context of the stars by which the church navigates, but then you must *fire*, or experiment. Only then, in this fast-paced culture, are you really able to *aim*. Vision, mission, and values are points fixed by the congregation, but the truth is even the stars are not permanently fixed in the heavens. With time, even they shift. The reality is that the work of creating an effective set of guiding principles is never finished and done. Even those "fixed" points must be open to change, growth, and adjustment as the sea we sail in continues to change.

Identifying core values and establishing a clear vision and a compelling mission should be a grassroots effort done with a process that includes the maximum number of people and gets the greatest level of buy-in. Once that is done, two additional steps are critical but often forgotten:

- A team should be established to ensure that the vision and mission are comprehensively communicated. Branding should reflect the new vision and should be so ubiquitous, consistent, and relentless that even the least active member knows what the vision is and what it looks like to express it in mission.
- An implementation team also is needed. This group should fearlessly ensure that the budget, staffing, bylaws, and governance/structure align to the current vision and mission. Failing to do this would be like trying to drive through Pennsylvania with a map of New York … when you have a GPS on your smart phone or in your car.

The shallow sea on which the ship of the church is sailing is tumultuous and the old maps simply aren't accurate anymore. The values, vision, and mission that can help us navigate are invaluable, but not remembering grace is a mistake the church has made too often. Things change, and we must, too. Besides, in a few years, these stars won't work for you anymore because the universe in which we live will have changed and you will need to do all this again.

LEADING CONGREGATIONS ON A WHITEWATER SEA

S eventeenth-century scientist Sir Isaac Newton observed in his first law of motion that "an object at rest stays at rest."[1] He might have drawn this conclusion while watching a pastor try to persuade a congregation to make some needed changes. Inertia, resistance, denial, and apathy can be much more aggressively powerful forces than their passivity implies. As baseball coach Jimmy Dugan (as played by Tom Hanks in the movie "A League of Their Own") says, "It's supposed to be hard. If it wasn't hard, everyone would do it. The hard is what makes it great." If change was easy, our churches already would have made the changes necessary for them to grow and thrive and be transformational forces. If it was easy, leadership wouldn't be necessary, and many jobs would be eliminated.

The Cathedral of Hope UCC began life as The Metropolitan Community Church (MCC) of Dallas. They were a part of a small denomination of mostly small congregations that sought to provide a safe spiritual haven for the lesbian, gay, bisexual, and transgender (LGBT) community at a time when no other churches were welcoming. In 1987, with 180 members, MCC Dallas was one of the larger churches in the denomination. In the face of many deaths caused by HIV/AIDS (eventually more than 1,500), it appeared that the church would face inevitable decline, but it did not. From 1987 until 2011 the church grew until its membership was more than 4,000, weekly attendance was more than 2,200, and its general fund budget was $4.5 million. They built a 900-seat sanctuary, a state of the art children's center, a national AIDS memorial, and the world-recognized Interfaith Peace Chapel.

The Cathedral of Hope became known as the world's largest LGBT church. It was, in fact, the largest progressive/inclusive church in the South and one of the largest and fastest growing in the world. It became a

---

[1] Isaac Newton, "Newton's First Law," Physics Classroom, http://www.physicsclassroom.com/class/newtlaws/Lesson-1/Newton-s-First-Law

liberal megachurch in Dallas, Texas. How? Members of the media came from around the world with the same question: "Why is the largest gay church in the world in Dallas, Texas?" That single congregation had a budget and staff greater than the denomination to which it belonged, which was part of the reason why, in 2003, it joined the United Church of Christ, where it still was one of the largest congregations, but at least had relative peers.

Rev. Elder Don Eastman was the pastor of MCC Dallas prior to 1987. He did a great job and left a strong church. Then, in the interim, AIDS hit that congregation, and 10 percent of its membership died in a single month. There was also an economic recession, which, in Dallas, became a depression. Everyone, including me, was shocked when, in the midst of those external circumstances, the church began to grow at a staggering rate. The Cathedral of Hope confirmed more than 300 new members in one year. In 2001, at a gathering of the pastors of the larger MCCs (all under 700 members, most under 300), Rev. Eastman led a workshop on church growth. At one point, he offered to explain why it was that the Cathedral of Hope accounted for 50 percent of the denomination's growth. This was an important moment because, frankly, I'd never been able to answer reporters' questions about why. Don is someone whose wisdom I trust, but I was disappointed when he explained that the secret to the phenomenon that was the Cathedral of Hope was "their capacity for reinvention."

He went on to say that it was a combination of the pastor's ability to reinvent himself in the face of challenges and change, and to lead the congregation to reinvent itself. Don explained that, at each developmental stage in the life of a church, the pastor has to function differently as does the congregation. "The reason most churches fail to thrive," he said, "is that the pastor lacks the courage to change or the skills to lead change."

At first, this did not seem to me to be an adequate explanation, but, over the years, working with many churches, it has proven remarkably astute. Fear is the enemy of change, and the greatest and most dangerous enemy lurks in the hearts of leaders who have grown comfortable and often competent with who they are and where they are. That is they are good at being the pastor of, say, a 150-member church but are afraid they might not be good at leading a larger church. There are no guarantees that change or reinvention will work. The one thing of which you can be certain is that often they will not. I often advise pastors that the only way their church will thrive is if they empower their staff and leadership to make mistakes.

Change isn't easy, and, though it does occur naturally in many settings, churches tend to consciously, or unconsciously, put systems and structures into place to resist change. Ironically, their resistance to change can be so great that they are willing to change leaders rather than embrace the lifegiving changes that are needed. Leaders underestimate the level of resistance to change at their own peril. This is why we all need to be trained to be change-agents if we are to be effective and long-term leaders.

It is tempting to believe that all we really need to do is explain the circumstances and people will do what is best for the Body. If you believe this then your doctor has never tried to get you to lose weight, stop smoking, exercise more, or worry less. We all know the facts. We've all seen people die because they failed to make these good and necessary changes. We love our children and grandchildren and want to live long and healthy lives. So, how easy has it been to change your diet, your work habits, or your sedentary lifestyle? We all have made changes, but soon fallen right back into bad patterns. Permanent changes are tough for individuals and churches. Perhaps remembering our own failures will make us more patient with our struggling congregation and keep us from unrealistic optimism about how difficult real and lasting change is. It can be done, but if it was easy everyone would do it.

So, here are seven secrets to successful transformation:

No Solos Allowed

A new or renewed leader almost always is the catalyst that initiates change. It is critical, however, that we understand the word "catalyst." Think of Jesus' example of yeast. A little can leaven the entire loaf, he said, but it does so from within and begins by transforming the dough immediately surrounding it.

The first stage in effectively leading change is recruiting leadership partners and helping them acquire the skills and insights necessary to take this perilous journey on an unknown, ever-changing sea with you. While you may have a clear vision of your destiny, the journey is unpredictable, and, when you sail into rough waters, you need a trustworthy crew that is fully prepared to do their jobs and keep the ship safe and on course. Again, it is not a question of IF you will hit resistance, but when. If you are the only one trained to sail the vessel then even small storms of resistance can throw you off course.

Recruit people who can be your natural allies and train them what to expect. No one should be surprised by resistance, and no one should take it personally if they know its true source. A team of well-trained leaders will find resistance to be a good sign that progress is being made and things are taking their natural course. Untrained partners tend to panic and add to the anxiety because they don't know want to expect. Your job is to recruit people who can be non-anxious presences in the congregation, the leaven in the loaf. Coach them to avoid didactic conversations and, instead, seek to inject a spirit of hopefulness that calms anxiety rather than promotes polarization, that encourages mutuality and civility.

In other words, you don't need a team of people to argue the case for change; you need partners that can help create a spirit of trust and hope and optimism in the community. It is more important that they understand the dynamics of change rather than the specifics of the change itself. As often as not, it isn't what you are proposing that is being resisted but change itself that is producing anxiety. The most significant influencers in a community can serve better as the non-anxious presence than as subject matter experts. In a storm most people don't need an explanation about thermodynamics; they need a calm and trusted voice to assure them that all will be okay. As you anticipate making vital changes, begin by identifying, recruiting, and training a small group of partners who will help you navigate the anxiety ahead. Done well, this will be one step you may later think you didn't need to take because the storms never became apparent or threatening. Neglect it, and the journey may be lost before you ever have a chance to sail out of the harbor.

Grieving the Myth

The myth that keeps most churches on the road to decline is that "healthy churches are free of conflict." That is a lie. Dying churches are free of conflict. Of course, this does not mean that conflict can't be unhealthy and kill a church, but we are called to be leaders for the living, not chaplains holding the hands of a dying church. In other words, your goal is NOT to keep everyone happy. The sooner you grieve and get over that myth the quicker you can get on with the changes that will save your church and empower it to save the hurting and hopeless in your community. Change brings inevitable conflict and chaos, but if you believe those things are not of God go back and read the Bible. Start with Genesis when God creates out of chaos.

Jesus did not send us into the world to "be nice." If conflict avoidance was the sign of a good person then Jesus was pure evil. If being conflict free is the sign of a healthy church, then the church in Acts was a complete failure. Conflict emerged the instant the church was born. "These are drunk with wine," was the accusation leveled at the church that was only minutes old. Already misunderstanding and accusation! Peter's first sermon was delivered in defense of the changes the Spirit was making in their midst. Although no one enjoys or deliberately seeks conflict, do not judge it as the absence of the spirit. When the Wind of God blows through, all manner of things get stirred up; do not mistake the chaos as being a failure of the Divine. It is, in fact, an opportunity for the Spirit to move across the face of the deep, creating something new and alive.

One of the things we all must make peace with is that change will create conflict, and conflict can be a gift of the Spirit. Our job as leaders is to remain non-anxious, remind the congregation that this is not the first time God's people have struggled with the dynamics of change, and reassure them that the God of rainbow, cloud, and fiery pillar still lives and will be with them on this journey. Some, perhaps many, will want to go back. As much as we want to keep everyone happy and everyone onboard, some inevitably will leave. Our job as leaders is to remember that the changes we are making are so others will join us and, thus, we will fulfill the call of God. Every long-term pastor can tell stories about how they lost a family or a group of members and feared the church would die, only to discover that their departure opened the door for others to join. It is not that the departing folks were wrong or bad, but their leave allowed for change that brought new growth. Every pastor squirms a bit when the lectionary reading comes around to John 15, and we are forced to deal with the idea of pruning for new growth. We all are trained and oriented to plant, water, and fertilize, but pruning is not in our DNA. As Jesus said, however, it is in God's nature, and who are we to resist the will of God?

As we prepare our churches for change, we also must prepare them for inevitable conflict. We must see it, as every healthy relationship also must, as an inevitable part of authentic love and growth. Our role as leaders is to facilitate the conflict as lifegiving and not allow it to become destructive and life-threatening. We must be the ones to:

- Speak the truth;
- Facilitate honest, healthy dialogue so all are heard;
- Keep a sense of humor alive;
- Constantly remember the ultimate goal;
- Keep hope alive;
- Remind everyone that God's call trumps our comfort (see Exodus); and
- Celebrate the victories and common joys.

There are consultants, coaches, therapists, and limitless resources that can help us learn to deal with the anxiety, resistance, and conflict that are inevitable with authentic change. Simply acknowledging that these are normal and healthy parts of sacred relationships is half the battle. How many marriages died premature deaths because couples were conflict avoidant for too long? Or because they thought healthy couples didn't fight? Or because one party simply repressed their feelings until it was too late to deal with them?

One of the greatest witnesses of the Bible is its honesty. Holy people disagree, conflicts are constant, and God works miracles through it all. Psychiatrist and bestselling author M. Scott Peck, in a lecture about relationships, said that there really are only two reasons for marriage: children and the friction. He contends that we cannot be healthy and whole people without the friction that comes from conflict and the change that it creates. Congregations are in covenant relationships with one another and with God. Friction is a healthy sign that the covenant is authentic, not superficial or artificially sweetened.[2]

Conflict is not only a natural result of change, but it is a catalyst for authentic change. Like leaven, you don't need too much, but some is essential. Otherwise, the dough will remain unchanged. Leaders must acquire the skills to help congregations navigate the stormy water, but, first and foremost, leaders must find the courage to sail into those waters. We must grieve the myth that "good churches don't fight." The truth is every relationship has conflicts, and healthy relationships are strong because of the changes that result from the conflict. Leaders cannot avoid conflicts, but they do cast the deciding vote for what they consequences are.

In his book *Managing at the Speed of Change*, change consultant Daryl R. Conner says, "Orchestrating pain messages throughout an institution is the first step in developing organizational commitment to change. No pain, no gain."[3] Leadership's critical role is helping congregations grieve the myths that are rooted in the past and in the fantasy that things aren't as bad as they seem. As parish consultant Dr. Lyle Schaller, one of my mentors, taught me, if we wake up and tomorrow is 1950 our churches are totally prepared to do vital and vibrant ministry. Our buildings are properly configured, our programming and priorities are perfectly aligned, and baby boomers are going to stream to our churches to raise their children with a proper Protestant education. However, if we wake up in the second decade of the 21st century, then almost everything is going to need to change.

There is a lot of grieving associated with the loss of the past in the one place that managed to hang on to it for half a century. Pastors can comfort and encourage people in their grief; however, it is critical that lay leadership speak the truth. Sooner or later, even the kindest and most compassionate doctor must tell the truth about a patient's condition and prognosis. My mother says that to know the truth but not tell it is the same

---

[2] M. Scott Peck, *A World Waiting to Be Born: Civility Rediscovered* (New York: Bantam Books, 1993), 105

[3] Daryl R. Conner, *Managing at the Speed of Change: How Resilient Managers Succeed and Prosper Where Others Fail* (New York: Random House, 1999), 99

as lying. Then she adds, "Christians don't lie." Well, my mother never tried to lead a church to renewal. Denial is treated as a sacrament, but it will not serve anyone well.

Tell the truth, challenge the myth, move ahead with hope. As with any other loss, there will be stages of grief, and one of those stages will be anger. Leadership means knowing that the anger isn't personal and accepting it as the price of truly leading. Speak the truth and do so in as many different ways as possible. Remember there are decades of denial to break through. Only once a congregation has worked through to acceptance is real change possible. Leaders are the first people who must grieve the congregation's mythology and accept the truth. Then it is their role to help the congregation do the same.

Creating a Sense of Urgency

John Kotter, a professor at Harvard's business school, in his book *Leading Change*, says that establishing a sense of urgency is a crucial first step to gaining needed cooperation.[4] He suggests that in a company with 100 employees at least a dozen must be motivated to go far beyond their routine efforts if change is to take effect. That number may be slightly high in voluntary organizations. It may be that 25 percent of the membership must get a sense of urgency in a church before change will begin to happen.

In an unpublished paper on "Leading Change in a Local Church," missionary church planter and college professor Dr. Greg Waddell refers to the necessity of "unfreezing" the system. He writes:

The most common mistake in change agency is to skip this step and introduce innovation before people recognize that they need it. This is like planting seed before plowing the earth or painting a car before applying the primer coat. There are things that have to happen or else the innovation will inevitably fail to take root. Leaders will almost certainly be faced with immediate and powerful resistance—similar to the physical body's natural immune system kicking in—if change is

---

[4] John P. Kotter, *Leading Change* (Watertown, Massachusetts: Harvard Business Review Press, 1996), 36

introduced without such preparation. Contrary to what some may think, change management does not consist merely of introducing change. Before the introduction of innovation, the old must first be unfrozen. The process of change begins with unfreezing the current situation and releasing the church from the forces that bind her, so she can respond effectively to her environment. So, how does this unfreezing take place? What can the leader do to unfreeze the congregation from its current configuration?

Creating a sense of urgency may be done in most situations by a frank description of the current situation and the resulting trajectory. Like a doctor doing a physical on a dying patient, the numbers speak the truth, especially when contrasted with the numbers of a healthy and thriving patient. In other, stronger situations, what needs to change might not be life-threatening, but changing it might be life-enhancing. For example, consider the way mental dexterity exercises have proven to retard mental decline in the elderly and those with Alzheimer's. It isn't that the person must change or die, but the quality of life and what the person can contribute are greatly enhanced by certain changes. Time and timing are critical factors in both situations, though. You cannot delay; lifestyle changes must take place now. With each passing day, the change is more difficult and the ultimate impact is diminished.

To continue with our sailing imagery, a sense of urgency is the place where the Wind of the Transforming Spirit meets our sails. The tension that is created becomes the power to move the ship along even when the seas become turbulent. The authors of the book *Leading Congregational Change* say that, "Urgency is critical in the individual congregation. It creates a driving force that makes the organization willing to accept change and to challenge the conventional wisdom."[5] The trouble, of course, is that most mainline denominations lack any sense of urgency. Perhaps this is where our interpretation of apocalyptic literature fails us. We have abandoned the message of urgency along with the understanding of historicity.

---

[5] Jim Herrington, Mike Bonem, and James H. Furr, *Leading Congregational Change: A Practical Guide for the Transformational Journey* (San Francisco: Jossey-Bass, 2000) 35

As agents of change, we are charged with the dual, and sometimes conflicting, roles of providing our congregations with enough hope and comfort to withstand the destructive forces of their anxiety, and enough tension to create a vibrant sense of urgency that something new must be born. Our role as midwives of change is both to calm and comfort the mother in the midst of perhaps the most painful experience of her life and urge her to push willfully for new life to be born.

In many settings, creating a sense of urgency requires a significant dose of truth telling, and we may need to begin with ourselves and our leadership. How do we have to change if we are to fully live into the mission of God for our lives and our church? Leadership that is willing to consider new possibilities without rushing to judgment may discover that the change that is needed begins in them. Nothing is more fascinating in the story of the early church than watching the leaders change as they sought to follow the wind of the Spirit as it blew across their world. They had to learn new ways of thinking and new ways of being as the Spirit brought people into the church that the early leaders never even knew existed.

Our sense of urgency must be driven by a newly energized passion for the lost and those who are dying without Christ. While that sentence might have been spoken by a Southern Baptist or some other evangelical, it is the passionate conviction of one who does not believe in a literal hell but who has walked with souls who live in a daily hell. Perhaps mainline pastors lack a sense of urgency because they spend too much of their time holding the hands of "nice people." If we don't believe that people need the grace and forgiveness and hope of the Gospels, then we have not had coffee with a single mother whose father told her that God was punishing her for getting pregnant out of wedlock. Our nice, pretty buildings are surrounded by tragedies and trauma and fear and desperate needs that we are called by Jesus to help. Hell is very real, and people right outside our doors can bear witness to its torment. Our churches lose their sense of urgency when they become so self-absorbed that the color of the new carpet in the parlor takes up more of our passion and time than how to help the homeless teenagers on our streets. Our job as spiritual leaders is to challenge people to care about the things that Jesus cared about so deeply that the threat of death itself would not deter him.

A crisis can create a sense of urgency, but, oftentimes, our churches are like the frog in the pot on which the temperature has been slowly and gradually raised. By the time we are aware of the threat to our lives, it is too late. In comfortably middle-aged and middle-class mostly-white churches the sense of social urgency also is absent. Mission trips and experiential ministry can help change that. Facilitating personal interaction with people in genuine need and crisis can help foster a sense of urgency. The bottom line is that we must move folks out of their comfort zones. If the threat is not personal or imminent, there will be little urgency, unless, of course, we can help a congregation fully embrace its identity as the Body of Christ. The best sense of urgency arises from an overwhelming need to live as Jesus would in the community in which God has placed them.

A Vision Powerful Enough to Transform

My definition of vision is nothing more than "articulating God's preferable future." Jesus taught us that we ought to pray for "God's reign to come; God's will to be done, on earth as it is in heaven." Clearly, we do not live in a world in which God's will is always done, so it is the subject of our prayers and our life's efforts. While it is presumptuous to claim to know the will of God in all matters, as disciples of Jesus, there are many ways in which God's will for humankind and for us is clear.

There have been a number of books written that suggest that the role of the modern pastor of a thriving church is principle visionary. God speaks to the senior pastor and through the senior pastor to the people of God. There is no doubt that this centralized and hierarchal model is efficient in certain settings and, by some standards, effective in mobilizing people to work toward a single goal. However, as Peter Senge, a senior lecturer at MIT, observed in his book *The Fifth Discipline*, "lofty visions alone fail to turn around a firm's fortunes."[6]

Dr. Fred Craddock, my preaching professor, often said, "Good preaching is not so much speaking to people as it is speaking for people." By that he meant that good preaching isn't when people are awed by the

---

[6] Peter Senge, *The Fifth Discipline: The Art & Practice of The Learning Organization* (New York: Doubleday, 1990) 12

preacher's wisdom and insight, but when they are allowed to discover their own. In the church a visionary leader is one who helps the people discover the vision for their church that they already treasure in their hearts and then to organize and articulate that vision back to them.

Leaders help a church ask:

- Who are we?
- What are we called to do?
- What Spirit-inspired dream burns in our hearts?
- Who would we be if all God's dreams for us came true?
- Who would we be if we were instruments in God's dreams for our community?

Churches can answer these questions for themselves, if given the opportunity. Hearing their vision in their own voice is powerful. It is also important because, if the vision is genuinely God-given, it will require a great number of changes and significant sacrifice. That is much more likely if it is THEIR vision than if you try to deliver it from on high. Leadership is facilitating the people to articulate their vision, and then helping them clarify it and develop a strategy around making it a reality.

Perhaps, as researcher and author Kirk Hadaway suggests, transformation vision is not so much showing people where they need to go, as it is helping them to see who they are and who they can be. Hadaway cites All Saints Episcopal Church in Pasadena and an example of how a progressive, radically-inclusive congregation was, and is, empowered by what he calls their "vow" rather than their "vision":

> *What they call their job and what I call a vow is this: On behalf of Jesus Christ to dismantle all structures of injustice. Dismantling injustice is not a vision or corporate goal—it is an intention and a direction that leads to specific actions. It is a vow, even a "covenant" with the world. Rather than following a vision, we give ourselves vision—the ability to see and then we act accordingly and resolutely.* [7]

---

[7] C. Kirk Hadaway, *Behold I Do a New Thing: Transforming Communities of Faith* (Bohemia, New York: Pilgrim Press, 2001)

That is powerful, but, as a strategy for change, vision may need to mean more than just that. For some of us, perhaps it just needs to be more fleshed out. The neuro-linguistic programming approach to communication, personal development, and psychotherapy is not without accurate criticism, but the way that it frames how different people are motivated can be insightful. For example, it describes how some people are "move-away-from" people and others are "move toward." Without judgment, it is simply an observation that some people are most powerfully motivated by their fears while others are motivated by possibilities. It is simply the old carrot/stick insight. Some people work really hard because they don't want to be poor. Some people work really hard because they want to be rich. The result in both cases is hard work, so one is not better than the other. Some people are spiritually motivated by hell/threat/danger; others are spiritually motivated by heaven/reward/promise.

I believe, and this is important to remember, that "one size fits some." You need to know which type you are and remember that not everyone is motivated in the same way you are. Some people will need you to clearly, consistently, and frequently paint a compelling picture of the preferable future into which God is calling your church. Others will need to hear, regularly and persuasively, an outline of the dangers posed by our failure to make the needed changes and answer the call of God. The vision will need to be visual, auditory, and kinesthetic. Everyone will need to see it, hear it, and feel it, but it will be more powerful for some in one form than the others.

John Kotter defines vision as "a picture of the future with some implicit or explicit commentary on why people should strive to create that future."[8] He also suggests three purposes that vision serves in a change process:

- Clarifying the direction for change. It allows the details of our journey together to be organized.
- Motivates people to take action in the same direction.

---

[8] Kotter, *Leading Change*, 68

- Coordinates the actions of individuals in a remarkably fast and efficient way.[9]

To that, I add a fourth. If it is the congregation's vision, and if it is fully owned, it will motivate the elimination of some of the organizational restraints. An externally compelling vision stands powerfully against the bureaucracy that physician, psychologist, philosopher, author, inventor, and consultant Edward de Bono defined as "an organization put together for a purpose, but coming to survive for its own sake."[10] To cut through these constraints the vision must be too powerful and compelling to be allowed to die of strangulation. Again, you will meet much greater success if a congregation has to choose between THEIR vision and THEIR organizational restraints.

You Can't Communicate Too Much

Change lives and dies by effective communication. It is imperative that the greatest number of people are involved in formulating the biggest picture. If the change is comprehensive, then every single member needs to be invited to participate from the start. This can be done in various ways, and, given people's schedules today, it probably needs to be done in a wide variety of ways. Ultimately, holding small groups in various places and at various times is probably most effective. It is impossible to ensure full participation in large gatherings. With a series of small group gatherings, you can ensure that everyone has the opportunity to attend. Then, by going around the room, every person is offered a chance to speak, though they may pass. Either way, the choice is theirs. Even if they pass, they are given a chance to email their thoughts. If the change redefines the future of the church it is imperative that no one feels they were not invited to participate.

Of course, once everyone has had a chance to have their say, your job will be to consolidate and organize their thoughts into a comprehensive

---

[9] Ibid. ch. 5

[10] Edward de Bono, *I am Right and You are Wrong: From This to the New Renaissance: From Rock Logic to Water Logic* (London: Penguin Books, 1991), 234

picture of God's preferable future. You probably will want to have your leadership team work through it with you, so they will feel some responsibility for how it was shaped. The final edit should be made by those who are most skilled and knowledgeable.

As the vision is formulated, you might think about concentric circles that move from the outside in. Once the vision is formulated, the strategy is developed from the inside out. Again, communication happens in concentric circles. Staff or mission-critical leadership should be fully briefed on all the strategic details. The larger the number to whom you are communicating the bigger the picture that needs to be communicated. Ultimately, you will need to be able to communicate the big picture for the future to those who know nothing about the church. It should be crafted to be so compelling that it would make those who do not know you want to find out more.

Until every single active member is sick of the vision you have not even begun to communicate with the larger community. In most churches the pastor is the chief communication officer, so it is her responsibility to work the message of transformation into every sermon, email, article, prayer, and announcement. He must be relentless and incredibly creative in how the message gets repeated. This will require enlisting the assistance of many different groups in the church. The team that works on internet communication likely will be very different from the one that produces printed material.

We tend to think of communication as the next stage in the process of change; however, it is also the catalyst that creates the change. On some levels, it also is the change itself. This is particularly true if the church is making a genuine paradigm shift in its identity. Michael Foss, Senior Pastor of Prince of Peace Lutheran church in Burnsville, Minnesota, did a great job documenting the process his congregation went through as they moved from membership to discipleship. Although there are a variety of reasons this particular shift wouldn't be appropriate for most progressive congregations, what is helpful is seeing how it happened and the transformations that took place along the way.

In his book *Power Surge,* (which is MUCH better than the title or cover would indicate) Pastor Foss talks about visiting DreamWorks in Hollywood, California and the Disney institute in Orlando, Florida. In both places, the thing that struck him was the vision of who they were, where they were going, and who they were to become along the way was communicated consistently and persistently. It is expressed again and again in every possible way, until it isn't memorized but rather integrated. The vision literally becomes a part of the fabric out of which the institution is made. Ultimately you CANNOT over-communicate. Foss writes:

> *Simply communicating the vision once, twice, or even thrice is not enough. We must plant the vision deep in the heart of the mission of the church and deep in the hearts of those who come to church. That is to say, we must weave it into the very fabric of our self-understanding as Christians. Purpose breeds personal power. The purpose of the Christian church—"faith active in love"—when connected to the lives of individual and family disciples is incredibly empowering.[11]*

When the people on the street know who your church really is and where it is going, then you will know that you have done an adequate job of communicating to your congregation. They literally must internalize it so it becomes a part of who they are. Moving a congregation toward a vision that has been that fully embraced is much easier because they are willing to change whatever it is that may be an impediment.

Root Change in Spiritual Practices

Please note that this is not a list of the seven steps of leading change. This is not the sixth thing that you do, nor is it the sixth most important thing that must be done. Some would suggest that this is the first and most important step. Churches that have used consultant and author Martha Grace Reese's *Unbinding the Gospel* series have found her suggestion to

---

[11] Michael W. Foss, *Power Surge: Six Marks Of Discipleship For A Changing Church* (Minneapolis: Fortress Press, 2000), 52

incorporate prayer throughout the process, perhaps beginning with a season of prayer, to be her most powerful point.[12]

Imagine for a moment the transformative power of asking the congregation to have no meetings of any kind for 90 days. Instead, they will spend that time fasting, praying, walking a labyrinth, worshipping using music from Taizé, and/or studying together. By the end of that period, in most churches, there would be a genuine spiritual awakening. There also would be a new awareness of what is really important and an openness to reconsidering how the congregation invests its time and energy.

While conflicts still will occur, because what is being changed is important and treasured, the disagreements are much less likely to be destructive when you have prayed together and heard one another's prayers as everyone earnestly seeks the will and wisdom of God. Sitting in silence and seeking the Spirit is a powerful reminder that we do not rely solely on our own wisdom, education, and experience. In the tender work of sensing the gentle breath of the Spirit, a migrant worker might be more skilled than a federal judge. In what other setting would one find the humility to listen to others with respect and grace?

Because most of the material contained in this book is designed for leaders of the congregation, and would be of little interest to those who simply are seeking to worship God, follow Jesus, and serve compassionately, I have not created a small group series to accompany it, though I do provide the basis for another in an appendix. There are, of course, dozens of excellent guides that will serve to help as many people in your congregation as possible to synchronize their hearts with the heart of God. By working through a spiritual exercise together the entire congregation, hopefully, will find a new openness to permitting and even helping the church be born again as a new, vibrant, and vital body doing the work of Jesus in your community. Leaders need their prayers, their patience, and their support. Leaders also need to take this spiritual journey with them. For this reason, every leader should be engaged in one of the small groups. This might mean that the staff and their partners gather one night a week to do the study, but it might be better for the leadership to be

[12] Martha Grace Reese, *Unbinding the Gospel: Real Life Evangelism 2nd Edition* (St. Louis: Chalice Press, 2008), part 4

in a group with others not leading the group, but journeying as one with the group.

The first step, of course, will be to train group leaders. Recruit the number of leaders that will be needed so that 75 percent of your congregation can participate. This may mean having groups meet at odd times or at times when child care is possible. After you have selected the leaders, ask them to recruit an assistant or apprentice. The idea is to train enough small group leaders for the future as the church and number of groups grows. Some of the groups will want to continue after the study, and that should be encouraged.

It is often easiest to start these groups as a Lenten discipline. It makes sense to ask everyone to study and prayer together following the model of the early church in preparation of Easter. The ultimate goal is spiritual resurrection for the congregation and rebirth for the church.

What is critical is to provide the spiritual underpinnings for the work of change. Prayer and fasting are important spiritual disciplines, but so is celebration. Don't forget that you gather every Sunday for the express purpose of celebrating the transforming work of God in the world and in human lives. Name this process as one of the ways in which God is expressly working in your midst. Give thanks and don't be afraid to name what is going on inside of you. While this is not about you, it is important for people to see that the leadership is fully sharing this experience—anxieties, hopes, and joys.

Don't forget, or let the congregation forget, that transformation/change is the *point* of the Christian faith. As the church works its way through the lectionary and liturgical cycle, it is remarkable to note how much of it speaks to renewal, change, and transformation. It is, after all, what Jesus came to do. While we progressives generally avoid the word "repent" because of its abuses, we must not forget that it, ultimately, is a word of good news. The idea that we and our congregations can repent is the ultimate testimony to the faithfulness and grace of God. Every person knows they need to make changes in their lives. We don't need to beat them up to persuade them to be different. What we do need is to offer them the opportunity to become the people they always have dreamed they could be, to repent, change directions, be transformed. That it is possible is the great good news of the redeeming grace of God.

Kirk Hadaway reminded us that the late social ecologist and business guru Peter Drucker who also was a man of faith said, "The business of the church is to **change** people; the business of a corporation is to **satisfy** them."[13] I would add that churches who get that backwards die and should. Churches that exist to satisfy their members have become closed clubs neglecting the mission of Jesus. Like the Dead Sea that seeks to retain all the water that flows into it, all life soon ceases to exist.

Transcendent worship, spiritual formation in community, and sharing one's self in service of compassion are the means by which the church is a catalyst for transformation. If people leave our worship unchanged, then we need to change our worship. If people are not transformed in small groups, then we need to give birth to different kinds of small groups. If the service ministries of our church aren't changing people's lives, then we need to find people with profound needs and learn from them.

Making changes in a church is hard work. Transforming religious people is so difficult it killed Jesus, but it is possible. You and I aren't the people we hope to be, but we aren't the people we once were either. We are different because we learned something, were deeply and repeatedly moved, met some people and became known by them, and were given an opportunity to help, give, and serve. These are the ways people are changed. Sometimes pain is the motivator, but pain and even the threat of death don't transform the human soul. That is a spiritual process, and the ministry of the church to help people go through that process in the same way Jesus did:

- He told them the truth and challenged them to change.
- He taught them and encouraged them.
- He led them into the presence of God.
- He gathered them into community and had them grow together.
- He sent them out to help and heal.
- He gave them hope of resurrection.

If the church can be the Body of Christ in these ways not only will it be transformed it also will be a transforming power in the world once more.

---

[13] Hadaway, *Behold I Do a New Thing*, 11

Develop Resilience

In *Managing at the Speed of Change,* Daryl Conner says, from start to finish, resilience is the key personality trait of successful leaders of change:

Wherever I went I recognized the same phenomenon—executives who were successfully implementing change, regardless of their location, displayed many of the same basic emotions, behaviors, and approaches ... I have determined that the single most important factor to managing change successfully is the degree to which people demonstrate resilience: the capacity to absorb high levels of change while displaying minimal dysfunction.[14]

Wikipedia offers a more traditional definition for "resilience":

Psychological resilience is defined as an individual's ability to successfully adapt to life tasks in the face of social disadvantage or other highly adverse conditions. Adversity and stress can come in the shape of family or relationship problems, health problems, or workplace and financial worries, among others. Resilience is the ability to bounce back from a negative experience with "competent functioning." Resilience is not a rare ability; in reality, it is found in the average individual and it can be learned and developed by virtually anyone. Resilience is a process, rather than a trait to be had. It is a process of individuation through a structured system with gradual discovery of personal and unique abilities.[15]

A common misconception is that resilient people are free from negative emotions or thoughts and remain optimistic in most or all situations. To the contrary, resilient individuals have, through time, developed specific coping techniques that allow them to effectively and relatively easily

---

[14] Conner, *Managing at the Speed of Change,* 6

[15] https://en.wikipedia.org/wiki/Psychological_resilience

navigate around or through crises. In other words, people who demonstrate resilience are people with optimistic attitudes and positive emotionality; they are, in practice, able to effectively counter negative emotions with positive emotions.[16]

The critical nature of resiliency in navigating on a whitewater, shallow sea is that changes come with greater speed and greater capacity for disruption in the culture. The church can embrace, navigate, and harness these changes, or seek to avoid and ignore them. While the latter option is greatly tempting, effective leaders know choosing that course leads inevitably to stagnation, decline, irrelevancy, and, ultimately, death for the institution. Too many churches believe that their longevity and sometimes large endowments inure them from the impact of these pervasive social changes; however, those things at best mask the symptoms until it is too late to change course. Remembering the lessons of the Titanic might serve us well as we sail through these constantly and tumultuously changing seas. Hubris is not a good substitute for resilience, though it too often passes for it in institutions and individuals.

Chapter 15 of Conner's book is entitled "Enhancing Resilience." As the title indicates, resilience is not an intransigent personality trait. George Bonanno, a clinical psychologist at Columbia University's Teachers College who has been studying resilience for 25 years, was quoted in an article in "The New Yorker" magazine as saying:

All of us share the same "fundamental stress-response system, which has evolved over millions of years and which we share with other animals. The vast majority of people are pretty good at using that system to deal with stress. When it comes to resilience, the question is: Why do some people use the system so much more frequently or effectively than others? One of the central elements of resilience, is perception: Do you conceptualize an event as traumatic, or as an opportunity to learn and grow?[17]

---

[16] "The Road to Resilience," American Psychological Association, http://www.apa.org/helpcenter/road-resilience.aspx

[17] Maria Konnikova, "How People Learn to Become Resilient," *New Yorker*, https://www.newyorker.com/science/maria-konnikova/the-secret-formula-for-resilience, (February 11, 2016)

Michael S. Piazza

The article's author, Maria Konnikova, goes on to say:

The good news is that positive construal can be taught. "We can make ourselves more or less vulnerable by how we think about things," Bonanno said. In research at Columbia, the neuroscientist Kevin Ochsner has shown that teaching people to think of stimuli in different ways—to reframe them in positive terms when the initial response is negative, or in a less emotional way when the initial response is emotionally "hot"—changes how they experience and react to the stimulus. You can train people to better regulate their emotions, and the training seems to have lasting effects.[18]

In other words, leaders can and must develop their own resiliency so that in the face of change, even traumatic change, we can help anxious people reframe the challenge to see the opportunity, possibility, and promise. This may be what the Bible calls "hope," and a primary obligation of church leaders is to be midwives of hope in an apprehensive community and in the world.

So, how do leaders develop and enhance their own resilience in the face of dramatic and persistent change?

University of Pennsylvania psychologist Martin Seligman has written about this in his book *Learned Optimism.* Seligman found that training people to change their explanatory styles from internal to external ("Bad events aren't my fault."), from global to specific ("This is one narrow thing rather than a massive indication that something is wrong with my life."), and from permanent to impermanent ("I can change the situation, rather than assuming it's fixed.") made them more psychologically successful and less prone to depression. He indicates that the cognitive skills that underpin resilience, then, seem like they can indeed be learned over time, creating resilience where there was none.[19]

---

[18] Ibid.

[19] Martin E. P. Seligman, *Learned Optimism: How to Change Your Mind and Your Life* (New York: Vintage Books, 2006)

80

This internal reframing transforms our own ability to experience the challenges of change with hope, but it is a vital skill if we are going to lead a community to do the same. George P. Lakoff, a professor of cognitive linguistics at the University of California, Berkeley is best known for his fascinating political book *Don't Think of an Elephant*. Dr. Lakoff says bluntly that, "If you keep their language and their framing and just argue against it, you lose because you are reinforcing their frame."[20] Or, if we allow those who are afraid of change or resistant to it to frame the issue for the congregation, the issue is foreordained regardless of how many facts you may have on your side.

When managing change, it is incumbent on us as leaders to determine the right frame for the change and articulate our arguments with moral authority within that frame. This is how hearts and minds are won … or lost. We must use the full range of communication tools. Facts are used to reinforce the legitimacy of our frame. Emotion is used to reinforce the morality of our frame. Symbols are used to improve the perception and immediate recall of our frame. I have found success by helping older or long-time members reframe their perceptions of what the church needs in terms of what their grandchildren might want or need if they are to reclaim the church. This is a process of tenaciously helping people think of an issue through the lens of their own, sometimes higher, values.

Resilient leaders are aware of their own points of resistance and pain, as well as the transformation of their own values. Then, from that place, they can help others find a way forward. It goes without saying that this is more effectively done before sides are drawn or conflict emerges. Perhaps what we should be considering is what I call "incremental pre-framing." By this I mean a confessional, incremental approach to change that is framed in the context of the stated values, mission, and vision of an organization. Returning to the parable of Virginia-Highland Church might give this specificity.

When I was in seminary, VHC was a 50-year-old Southern Baptist church located in a transitional neighborhood. The city of Atlanta had decided to put a freeway through the neighborhood, one block from the

---

[20] George Lakoff, *The ALL NEW Don't Think of an Elephant!: Know Your Values and Frame the Debate* (White River Junction, Vermont: Chelsea Green Publishing, 2014), 28

church. Houses were purchased, and two dozen older exquisite craftsman homes were demolished. By the time the parkway was halted by their neighbors, half the membership of Virginia-Highland Church had fled to the suburbs. Because of that sudden and precipitous decline, the church voted to ordain women in the congregation as deacons. This happened just as the fundamentalists were taking over the Southern Baptist Convention, so the church's decision resulted in them being kicked out. Later, a decision to welcome lesbian, gay, bisexual, and transgender people precipitated their disfellowship from the Georgia Baptist Convention. Ultimately, they affiliated with the United Church of Christ.

By the time I became their pastor in 2011, they had declined to the point of imminent closure, so radical and rapid change was required. Although they called me because of my reputation for congregational renewal, it was clear from the beginning that what they really wanted was for things to be fixed but nothing to be changed. One strategy might have been to leverage my "expertise and experience" to persuade them that I really did know what was needed. That likely would have been a losing strategy in this very congregational setting. My two-fold approach was to leverage their pain (the very real threat of the loss of their building and church) and remind them of their values, vision, and history.

Every proposed change was framed in the context of their DNA as a church of radical inclusion, courage, and progressive values. It also was explained in terms of the consequences of failing to make the proposed change. I repeatedly invited them to experiment and give change a chance because that kind of entrepreneurial courage was their heritage. We lost members who were reluctant to give up control, but the changes began to attract new, younger, and more diverse members. We celebrated that fact with such intensity that the losses barely were noticed. Time and again I affirmed them for living out of their courageous past and into the vision and values of their future. At one point, one change-resistor caught on and said, "We never would have let you read our history if we had known you would use it against us." In the end, by framing changes as an expression of their own history and values, the resistance was small and short-lived in what had been labeled "a troubled and difficult church."

The resilience for this came from my knowing that they had asked me to save the church, so, like a doctor who must amputate a limb to save a patient, I did not take their limp personally. I also would not let them attach the changes NOR the credit for the growth to me. As someone wise once said, "If we fail it is my fault, but if we succeed it is theirs." Hence, we acknowledged failures briefly, but celebrated successes relentlessly, which reframed a legacy of decline into a promise of success.

CONGREGATING ON A SHALLOW SEA

Historically, churches have gathered in three ways: in worship, as congregations (the core membership), and in small groups. Each of these divisions had different expressions, but they were relatively consistent across denominational lines. Of course, churches with a congregational form of governance gathered more often as the middle-sized core membership, but I worked with one United Methodist church in which 300 people attended the annual "Charge Conference," and 120-140 came to their monthly administrative board/council on ministries meetings.

In many Southern Baptist churches Sunday school (small group) attendance often exceeds worship attendance, though that trend has changed in the past decade or so. As the Cathedral of Hope grew into a small megachurch, we consciously eliminated the middle group. The current facility was designed to seat almost 1,000 people and host at least two services every Sunday. The "fellowship hall," however, has a capacity of fewer than 100 and was designed to be overflow space for worship. It connects to a large narthex so the two, together, can hold 500 standing people after worship for coffee hour. With more than 4,000 members and 2,200 in worship during the week at its height, even the sanctuary would not accommodate an authentic congregational gathering.

The Cathedral was a regional church with members who attended from throughout the Dallas/Fort Worth Metroplex, with some even commuting by plane each Sunday. This forced us to think of church, community, congregation, fellowship, education, and spiritual formation differently. Today, all churches face this reconsideration. What does Christian education look like when younger adults do not attend classes and those who do are aging rapidly? How do you offer fellowship, make connections, and build community when members' lives are too frantic to attend traditional functions like women's/men's groups, potlucks, or even choir practice? How can you do spiritual formation when your most active members attend only 50 percent of the time and most attend only about 12 Sundays a year?

This shallow sea reality is masked, or at least moderated, in most mainline churches because more than 60 percent of those who attend worship are over the age of 50, and more than one-third are over the age of 65.[1] The older demographic remains the most consistent in their attendance; however, as that demographic also is closest to death, the reality of frequent worship attendance also is passing away. In new or renewed churches like Virginia-Highland Church, the fact that they succeed in attracting younger people forces them to address this reality sooner and more comprehensively. That church utterly lacked the demographic that attends church almost every Sunday. Of course, this point was made earlier in the book, but there are two reasons for reemphasizing it here.

First, the seismic implications of this shift take a while to comprehend and internalize. We who have been involved in church for a long time—some of us even for our entire lives—are slow to anticipate the impact this shift is having and will have on the institution we love. Consultants, academicians, and judicatory leaders often elucidate the reasons for the decline in church attendance. Reduced frequency, however, rarely makes the list, yet it explains so much. We talk a great deal about the "nones" and those who are "spiritual but not religious" without recognizing that there are millions who are spiritual AND religious but simply are expressing it differently.

The other reason for our return to this subject is that we must begin to explore and experiment with new ways of being church for those who would like to be spiritual and religious but for whom traditional ways of doing church simply do not fit their present reality. We have explored a few ways to enliven worship that might attract younger people, and we have talked about using technology to monitor and address the challenge of decreasing frequency. Given the irreversible shifting currents in the cultural sea on which we sail, however, it is imperative that we also explore new ways to shape the spiritual formation of people who do not

---

[1] Michael Lipka, "Which U.S. religious groups are oldest and youngest?" Pew Research Center, http://www.pewresearch.org/fact-tank/2016/07/11/which-u-s-religious-groups-are-oldest-and-youngest/ (July 11, 2016)

read the Bible, do not attend worship frequently (two or more times a month), and for whom Sunday school and other traditional forms of religious education hold no appeal.

So, what might spiritual formation look like in a church on a shallow sea? My research on this topic produced very limited results, so most of my conclusions are drawn from congregations I have pastored and churches with whom I have consulted. The lack of data is unsurprising because most churches still are redoubling their efforts to make old models work. Churches like Virginia-Highland, for whom old models no longer existed (they had no programs when I arrived) were forced to invent new ones. These are experiments designed to see what is effective and what is not in this new age. One key to experimental leadership is the awareness that you will not discover a solution. At best, you will find something that works for some people, some of the time, for a while. Given the everchanging, whitewater nature of a shallow sea, one should not expect to find a new way of doing spiritual formation, but should discover and create a culture and system that is evolving.

Another core principle is that technology must be an ally in these experimental programs. While "spiritual growth" may seem impossible to measure, we need to set goals and objectives, and we must fearlessly evaluate and measure. Remember: what you measure grows because it forces you to invest in it with integrity.

The final core principle in finding new ways to do spiritual formation is doing it for better/stronger reasons. My 85-year-old mother has been a member of the same Sunday school class for almost half a century. My 87-year-old father quit years ago and, instead, works as a volunteer in their small-town United Methodist Church during that time. He asked, "Why doesn't anyone ever graduate from Sunday school?" While he simply may have gotten tired of the hard chairs the class sits on, his question is the correct one.

In many settings, people were coerced to learn about the Bible and church doctrine because, well, because that is what good people did. Because the Bible, like the Koran, too often has been abused to justify war, slavery, and the oppression of women and lesbian, gay, bisexual, and transgender people, a new generation can find little motivation to study a 2,000-year-old document. In my experience, the higher the value a church places on scripture the higher the chances that people at the margins are not welcome as beloved children of God. This has been a cornerstone for the growth of the "spiritual but not religious" movement. It isn't that they are abandoning God or disavowing a spiritual life, but the all-too-visible abuses of fundamentalism in all three Abrahamic religions have driven away younger people.

So, why should we offer and support spiritual formation? What would motivate them to trust us to "form" their spiritual lives? Answering these two questions should shape what we offer and how we offer it.

Millennials are motivated to volunteer and get involved in projects and activities that have *impact* on our world. The Case Foundation's "Millennial Impact Report" discovered that, although millennials don't tend to call themselves "activists," viewing the word as "too militant," their behavior reveals that they are classically just that. They prefer the word "advocate," but, "Millennials we interviewed wanted to give all people—but especially marginalized or disenfranchised individuals or groups—early interventions and opportunities that would ensure increased prosperity in life." [2]

"Advocating" for and working with the marginalized and disenfranchised long have been specialties of many vintage mainline churches. In the name of modesty or humility, we have done a terrible job of letting those outside the church know how well we do these things. Many of the churches I work with do not even let their own members know. Plymouth UCC in Lawrence, Kansas discovered that many of their members were unaware that they had housed, supported, and funded the oldest Head Start program in the country for decades. Many discovered it only when the President of the United States visited the program and commended it.

We talked previously about how our churches must become the "charity of choice" by quantifying and reporting how much good we do at the lowest possible cost. Recruiting millennials to join our efforts to

[2] Cindy Dashnaw, "The Millennial Impact Report: Phase 1: Millennial Dialogue on the Landscape of Cause Engagement and Social Issues," http://www.themillennialimpact.com/sites/default/files/reports/Phase1Report_MIR2017_060217.pdf, 8

change the world is another major reason for tracking, tabulating, and reporting this. Young "advocates" might be willing partners in our efforts, giving us an opportunity to befriend them and demonstrate the values that our brand of Christianity holds. My two millennial daughters both have reported on a number of occasions that their friends are not hostile to the church but simply have no idea who we are or what we do. When they invite their peers to volunteer activities they report that they are touched that so many "older people" care so deeply and have for so long.

Rather than seeking to create classes or worship that will provide spiritual formation for the next generation, we might consider leading with our advocacy, social justice, and community service work. In this regard, however, we cannot simply neglect the spiritual formation. For example, in one church that is attracting younger members, more than 100 people gathered every morning to work in the community food pantry. This ministry was hosted by a church from another denomination, and the group gathered in the chapel 10 minutes early to "get their assignments." They were welcomed by the coordinator who spoke very briefly about why s/he was so proud of them and how this was an expression of the values of Jesus and a manifestation of the Body of Christ on Earth. S/he then would ask those gathered if they minded if s/he led them in prayer. S/he would begin by giving thanks for the many altruistic people gathered, then pray for the sisters and brothers they would serve, and finished by asking the God of mercy and compassion to continue to motivate and empower them to be Christ's risen body on Earth.

After a few weeks, the regular churchgoers reported that the young people with no church background who joined them began to ask question about the church. Members would invite them to Sunday worship and go to brunch after the service with some of their friends. Perhaps it was merely the prospect of free food, but many of them began to appear in the pews.

The point, of course, is that we must find new ways to practice our faith assertively. The classic progressive Protestant reticence to pair their service with a spiritual explanation must change. If we do not provide spiritual context for our activities the church is simply another charity, and we cannot expect those who do not know us to care about the institution or their own spiritual lives. The evangelical church calls this "witnessing" and "evangelism," but in mainline Protestant churches those generally are regarded as four-letter words. Although we don't need to proselytize or impose our faith on anyone, acting as though we are embarrassed by it serves no one. Teaching our own members to "come out" as people of faith BECAUSE of our values and our desire to *widen the welcome* can reform insiders spiritually and might invite the "nones" to reconsider the possibilities. Failing to do so is as passively excluding as the days when people of color or LGBT folks were not welcomed to our churches.

Ministry-based spiritual formation is one way to build a sense of community while fueling and forming a congregation's spirituality. Another approach that seems to work well with millennials and those seeking to reclaim faith is traditional spiritual disciplines and practices. Many have found Buddhism attractive precisely because they see its focus on practice rather than doctrine or theology. Too many have seen church conflict and division about theological issues, and want no part of it. When practiced individually in community, rather than in isolation, contemplation, meditation, prayer, fasting, keeping the Sabbath, walking the labyrinth, worship, service, generosity, gratitude, etc. have a powerful attraction.

The 2015 *Washington Post* article by Rachel Held Evans I referenced in the chapter on worship stimulated a great deal of conversation by its title alone: "Want millennials back in the pews? Stop trying to make church 'cool.'" Evans quoted evangelical researchers from the Barna group, and I sometimes find their research suspect because of their stated agenda and theology. More compellingly, Held also quoted two of her fellow millennial bloggers:

My friend and blogger Amy Peterson put it this way: "I want a service that is not sensational, flashy, or particularly 'relevant.' I can be entertained anywhere. At church, I do not want to be entertained. I do not want to be the target of anyone's marketing. I want to be asked to participate in the life of an ancient-future community."

Millennial blogger Ben Irwin wrote: "When a church tells me how I should feel ('Clap if you're excited about Jesus!'), it smacks of inauthenticity. Sometimes I don't feel like clapping. Sometimes I need to worship in the midst of my brokenness and confusion — not in spite of it and certainly not in denial of it."[3]

It was my experience at the Cathedral of Hope and Virginia-Highland Church that "nones," the post-churched, young couples with children, LGBT people, and millennials were fascinated with, motivated by, and attracted to enlivened vintage worship, rigorous spiritual challenges, and devotion-deepening communal practices. Both of these congregations grew and thrived by making traditional Christian worship and practices relevant to the lives of younger people living fully present in the 21st century. That, of course, is very different than a church continuing to do things the same way they did in the 1950s.

Perhaps the church has been too apologetic about the challenges it is called to issue. We have become therapeutic and try to help people learn to accept themselves. The Gospel calls us to "deny self." Churches that challenge the pervasive value system often find a community that appreciates that. One group of parents I encountered explained that one of the reasons they brought their kids to worship was that the church hoped to save them from growing up to be "narcissistic, materialistic assholes."

Millennial author Brent McCraken, in his book *Uncomfortable: The Awkward and Essential Challenge of Christian Community*, wrote:

If the church is going to thrive in the twenty-first century, she needs to be willing to demand more of her members. She needs to assert the importance of covenants over comfort, even if that is a message that will turn off some. She needs to speak prophetically against the perversions of cultural and consumer Christianity, seeker unfriendly as that will be. She needs to call Christians away from an individualistic, "just me and Jesus" faith, challenging them to embrace the costliness of the cross and the challenge of life in a covenantal community.[4]

Becka Alper, a researcher with the Pew Research Center, posits that millennials are just as spiritual as older Americans, but not as religious. She writes:

While Millennials are not as religious as older Americans by some measures of religious observance, they are as likely to engage in many spiritual practices. For instance, like older Americans, more than four-in-ten of these younger adults (46%) say they feel a deep sense of wonder about the universe at least once a week. Likewise, most also say they think about the meaning and purpose of life on a weekly basis (55%), again, similar to older generations. Roughly three-quarters of Millennials feel a strong sense of gratitude or thankfulness at least weekly (76%). And 51% say they feel a deep sense of spiritual peace and well-being at least once a week. By comparison, older Americans are only slightly more likely than Millennials to say they feel a strong sense of gratitude. Only when it comes to feeling spiritual peace and well-being are members of these four older generations more likely than Millennials to answer in the affirmative. Furthermore, on some traditional measures of religious belief, the difference between Millennials and older Americans is not that large.[5]

In *Finding Faith: The Spiritual Quest of the Post-Boomer Generation,* Richard Flory and

Donald Miller report on a study of churches that are engaging emerging adults (what they call "Post-Boomers") and the experience of

---

[4] Brent McCraken, *Uncomfortable: The Awkward and Essential Challenge of Christian Community,* (Wheaton, IL: Crossway, 2017), 183

[5] Becka A. Alper, "Millennials are less religious than older Americans, but just as spiritual," Pew Research Center, http://www.pewresearch.org/fact-tank/2015/11/23/millennials-are-less-religious-than-older-americans-but-just-as-spiritual/, (November 23, 2015)

these young adults in their churches. They observe that these emerging adults have "embedded their lives in spiritual communities in which their desire and need for both expressive/experiential activities, whether through art, music, or service-oriented activities, and for a close-knit, physical community and communion with others are met."[6]

Flory and Miller characterize Post-Boomer faith as "expressive communalism, in which Post-Boomers are seeking spiritual experience and fulfillment in community and through various expressive forms of their spirituality, both private and public."[7]

John Roberto, managing Editor of "Lifelong Faith," a quarterly journal on the theory and practice of lifelong faith formation, has used Miller and Flory's research extensively, and describes Post-Boomer faith as "reflecting an emphasis on embodiment and community: using one's body in worship; in living out, or embodying, Christian teachings, in service; and in a desire for life in a particular faith community where they can be both personally fulfilled and serve others."[8] He says that those who are reclaiming the faith desire a theologically grounded belief that is rational and an embodied spiritual experience.

Using Miller and Flory's research as his guide, Roberto goes on to recommend that churches who want to reach millennials should:

- *offer community and spirituality in the context of a clearly defined faith tradition*
- *offer worship and faith formation that is visual and experiential*

---

[6] Richard Flory and Donald Miller, *Finding Faith: The Spiritual Quest of the Post-Boomer Generation*, (New Brunswick, NJ: Rutgers University Press, 2008), 189

[7] Ibid, 17

[8] John Roberto, "Research-based Practices for Shaping Faith Formation across the Life Span," *Lifelong Faith*, https://www.lifelongfaith.com/uploads/5/1/6/4/5164069/__ctr_for_congregations_-_research-based_practices_handout.pdf, 4

- *respond to their needs for empowerment, leadership opportunities, responsibility, and accountability, as well as authenticity and accessibility*
- *strengthen their distinctive Christian identity so that they know who they are and what they believe, and are able to honestly encounter religious differences, understand people of other faiths, and explore areas of mutuality*
- *provide opportunities for serving the surrounding community, "bringing the*
- *church to the community"*
- *study the Bible and Christian tradition, then apply it to life in an environment that promotes relationship building and encourages questioning*
- *engage them in creative uses of the history, traditions, and rituals of different Christian traditions for a more physically and visually oriented practice; and encouraging the development of ancient spiritual disciplines, such as silence and contemplation.*[9]

It has been my experience that many unchurched people are not hostile or resistant to the church but are simply uninformed about who we are and what we do. They deeply value religious traditions that are explained, taught, and offered in such a way that makes sense to them and is relevant to their lives or to their families. While individualism plagues this age, there also is a value for authentic vulnerable relationships, public space, and covenants that fill a gap left by the diaspora of families. The church can leverage all of these to build a spiritually thriving congregation, but the first step is understanding what people need and seeking and relinquishing our practice of judging one generation by another's standards.

In *Lost and Found: The Younger Unchurched and the Churches that Reach Them*, Ed Stetzer, Richie Stanley, and Jason Hayes, report on the findings from three LifeWay Research projects, including a large-scale survey of young adults and a survey of 149 churches that were reaching an extraordinary number of young adults. Based on what they gleaned

---

[9] Ibid. 4-5

94

from these presumably evangelical churches, the authors found nine common denominators for churches that were effective in impacting the spirituality of young adults.[10] Each of these factors is the basis of a chapter in the third part of the book and were summarized in a "Bookbrief" for the Union Baptist Association of Houston:

1. ***Creating Deeper Community.*** *Churches that are effective at attracting and developing young adults place a high value on moving people into a healthy small group system. Young adults are trying to connect and will make a lasting connection wherever they can find belonging.*
2. ***Making a Difference through Service.*** *Churches that are transforming young adults value leading people to serve through volunteerism. More than being pampered, young adults want to be part of something bigger than themselves and are looking to be part of an organization where they can make a difference through acts of service.*
3. ***Experiential Worship.*** *Churches that are engaging young adults are providing worship environments that reflect their culture while also revering and revealing God. More than looking for a good performance, young adults desire to connect with a vertical experience of worship.*
4. ***Conversing the Content.*** *Churches that are led by authentic communicators are drawing young adults into the message. Though their styles vary from topical to exegetical, authentic communicators are true to their own personal style of communication and are usually more conversational than preachy.*
5. ***Leveraging Technology.*** *Churches that are reaching young adults are willing to communicate in a language of technology familiar to young adults. Young adults sense that these churches are welcoming churches that value and understand them, engaging them where they are.*

---

[10] Ed Stetzer, Richie Stanley, and Jason Hayes, *Lost and Found: The Younger Unchurched and the Churches that Reach Them*, (Nashville: B&H Publishing Group, 2009)

6. ***Building Cross-Generational Relationships.*** *Churches that are linking young adults with older, mature adults are challenging young adults to move on to maturity through friendship, wisdom, and support. Young adults are drawn to churches that believe in them enough to challenge them.*

7. ***Moving Toward Authenticity.*** *Churches that are engaging young adults are reaching them not only by their excellence but by their honesty. Young adults are looking for and connecting to churches where they see leaders that are authentic, transparent, and on a learning journey.*

8. ***Leading by Transparency.*** *Churches that are influencing young adults highly value an incarnational approach to ministry and leadership. This incarnational approach doesn't require revealing one's personal sin list so much as it requires that those in leadership must be willing to express a personal sense of humanity and vulnerability.*

9. ***Leading by Team.*** *Increasingly churches reaching young adults seem to be taking a team approach to ministry. They see ministry not as a solo venture but as a team sport—and the broader participation it creates increases the impact of the ministry.*[11]

Many churches are using small groups to do Christian education. These groups are facilitated by a member, not taught by a leader. Millennials will seek small groups that respect millennial values. Studies show that millennials commonly value authenticity, being known, truth, and purpose/impact. **Millennials will not engage in groups that feel disingenuous to them. Authenticity is valued more than quality.** If they sense you are using small groups to sell them values or indoctrinate them, they will opt out. They want faith to connect to their lives as they are and empower them to make it and the world better. For this reason, connecting small groups to social service activities can be most effective. Reflection–action and action-reflection is a rhythm that works in many

---

[11] UBA Staff, "Bookbrief: Lost and Found: The Younger Unchurched and the Churches That Reach Them," UBA Houston, http://www.ubahouston.org/resources/media/book-notes/lost-and-found--the-younger-unchurched

settings. Simply doing good work makes the church just like any other worthy charity. It is the reflection that puts the work in context and helps to connect the values expressed to the values of faith.

Given the reality of the shallow sea on which the church must sail, learning to do spiritual formation digitally is probably a necessity, and using technology more frequently and effectively may help reach millennials and gen-Xers. Since shortly after the 2004 election, when the term "values voter" became synonymous with conservative candidates using hot button issues to turn out conservative Christian voters, I have been writing a daily "devotion" called *Liberating Word*. It has become a substantial tool for keeping connected with people who attend worship with decreasing frequency, though it was not intended for this purpose. On a number of occasions, I have been in the community and had people who I did not know or who did not attend church frequently enough for me to recognize them, come up and call me "pastor." One man was gracious enough to explain that there was no reason for me to recognize him, but we had been sending him *Liberating Word* since visiting the church only once. He regarded me as his pastor and our church has his spiritual home, even though he did not attend. (He did note that he sent a little money now and then.)

In their program resources, the Social Media Chaplaincy Corps: Worldwide Mission, an online resource, suggests a plethora of specific recommendations, including this:

> *Utilize digital media to exploit the potential of the learning opportunities available through online resources and networks. We live in a digital age of a media-rich, networked world of infinite possibilities. Digital media promotes engagement, self-directed learning, creativity, and empowerment by using the Internet, computers, iPods and iPads, smart cell phones, and many other digital tools to learn and communicate in ways that were not possible in previous generations. Today's children, teens, and young adults smoothly and seamlessly dive into new Web 2.0 communication technologies. With a flick of the cell phone, they share more texts, photos, music, and video than any other demographic group on Earth. Digital media allows learners to be active creators and producers who*

use a wide range of digital tools to express themselves, interpret the world around them, and deepen their understanding of academic content. Their products include original music, animation, video, stories, graphics, presentations, and Web sites. They can become actively engaged in their learning processes rather than passive recipients of knowledge. They can actively collaborate in many new ways in the digital, virtual world, an environment parallel to the traditional one of face-to-face interaction. Given their fluency with digital tools, today's youth and young adults become teachers for younger and older generations. They maintain content-rich Web sites, share favorite resources, lead online workshops and classes, and develop multimedia products designed to share their knowledge with others. This teaching role enables young people to gain confidence and reinforce their own learning, because the best way to learn something is to teach it.[12]

Because virtually every laptop, cell phone, and tablet has video and audio capabilities, virtual group gatherings are accessible almost anywhere to almost everyone. Touching a generation who uses this technology daily in their work or education only makes sense. In urban settings where distance, and more often traffic, makes it very difficult to get home, tend the kids/pets, and get to a class, meeting, or group gathering, virtual community is increasingly important. Technology such as Zoom, Go-to-Meeting, and Facebook Live makes it possible for every church to do this. The only incumbrance is generational. Older members resist or disdain virtual gatherings because they value being with others face-to-face. This is probably rooted in the fact that they are no longer going to work every day, or their once busy home is now quiet and their "nest" empty. Younger people who still are working, commuting, and often starting families end up excluded by how traditional churches too often do their programming and ministry. Technology can be leveraged to at least partially fill that gap. It is hubris for one generation to devalue the needs and experiences of another. While older members may not find virtual gatherings intimate,

---

[12]http://socialmediachaplaincycorp.blogspot.com/p/hurchwide-spiritual-formation-program.html

many young people are quite adept at using social media to maintain their most valuable and intimate relationships.

Virginia Theological Seminary has developed extensive resources for local churches and has a website, DigitalLiteracyToolkit.org, devoted to 21st-century skills and resources for ministry. In the December 2016 issue of *Trends*, a virtual magazine for the training industry, Doug Harward talks about how corporate trainers must begin to understand how technology is shaping the ways that future employees learn. This is a lesson that the church neglects at its own peril. He notes, "The evolution of gaming theory has found that using the principle of storytelling and engagement is key to appealing to learner emotions while enhancing learner engagement and recall."[13] It is ironic that a faith based on sacred storytelling and engagement, has missed this evolution almost entirely. "Digital faith formation" is a new concept for most of us, but there are extensive resources already developed that can assist us.

The goal of spiritual formation is not to get people into the building that the church owns. If we hope to shape the values and life-vision of future generations, the church must constantly innovate, adapt, and experiment. We must find new ways, reinvigorate old ones, and reconsider our objectives for building the spiritual vitality of people who are children of God, even if we don't seem them as often as we once did or would prefer. This reality makes this work more vital than ever.

One church that models virtual faith formation is Zion Church in Landover, Maryland. Founded by Rev. Keith Battle in February of 2000, the church now reports more than 5,000 people in worship and thousands more who worship though live stream from one of their three suburban Washington, D.C. locations. They stream each Sunday at 8, 9:45, and 11:30 a.m. and, 3, 7, and 9 p.m. The church also makes extensive use of small groups to keep the expansive congregation connected.[14]

---

[13]Doug Harward, "Innovation in Educational Planning," https://www.trainingindustry.com/magazine/nov-dec-2016/key-trends-for-2017-innovation-in-educational-technology/, Nov./Dec. 2016

[14] Will Johnston, "Clearing the Way for Small Groups," http://www.smallgroups.com/articles/2016/clearing-way-for-small-groups.html, (February 22, 2016)

The most remarkable use of technology at Zion, however, might be the way they keep their children connected virtually to their "Xtreme Kidz Children's Church." Zion recognized a phenomenon that most other congregations also are experiencing. Because adults attend less consistently, so do their children. This is further exacerbated by the increased number of divided households. The majority of children today live in two homes with different parents in different locations.[15] This often results in children's attendance being even less consistent than adults.

Zion Church has created a site, xtremelive.zionicampus.com, dedicated to resourcing kids, teaching them lessons consistent with the themes taught on campus, and equipping parents to be involved in supporting the spiritual formation of their children. While their introductory music and other elements are professionally produced, most of the content can be created by any church. Don't believe me? Consider that a film shot entirely with an iPhone and a $8 app received great acclaim at the Sundance Film Festival.[16] Editing software is included on many laptops, and there are young members in many churches just asking to be put to work on a project like this. The short segment of your children's lesson can be used in the classroom, posted on YouTube, Vimeo, and/or your church's website, and a link can be sent to every parent in the church encouraging them to share it with their children so they won't be behind when they return to Sunday school. This also can serve to remind kids what a great time they have at church and motivate them to ask their parents to take them back.

This is but one example of what one church is doing with technology to enhance the spiritual formation of their congregation. Today, the greatest limit is failure of imagination and our insistence that church happens only when people are in the building that we mistakenly call "the

---

[15] "The Majority of Children Live With Two Parents, Census Bureau Reports," https://www.census.gov/newsroom/press-releases/2016/cb16-192.html, (November 17, 2016)

[16] Casey Newton, "How one of the best films at Sundance was shot using an iPhone 5S," https://www.theverge.com/2015/1/28/7925023/sundance-film-festival-2015-tangerine-iphone-5s, (January 28, 2015)

church." Technology is so inexpensive now that many young people know how to do things we only dreamed of just 10 years ago. Small camcorders produce quality video and provide editing capabilities that fit in the palm of one's hand. When the Cathedral of Hope began its television and Internet ministry the cost of equipment was more than $500,000. The cameras were too large to put on standard tripods, and the editing equipment filled what could have been a large classroom. Today, the equipment is smaller, dramatically cheaper, and better, and it is simple enough to use that it affords volunteers new opportunities for ministry.

American moral and social philosopher Eric Hoffer said, "In a time of drastic change it is the learners who inherit the future. The learned usually find themselves equipped to live in a world that no longer exists."[17] The Catechetical Office of the Archdiocese of New York hosted what they called a "Digital Discipleship Boot Camp" to train Roman Catholic churches to begin using technology in their confirmation process. The mission of the organization within the church that is offering these boot camps to train-the-trainers is "to inspire, train and equip Catholic ministers to become lifelong learners and evangelizers with New Media."[18] It is imperative that vintage churches become learners themselves and relinquish the idea that we know how to do spiritual formation, Christian education, discipleship, and congregation building. This is an area of great opportunity for us to learn, so we can teach and reach the next generation of God's children.

---

[17] Eric Hoffer, *Reflections on the Human Condition*, (New York City: Harper & Row, 1973)

[18] "Digital Discipleship: Lifelong Learners in the New Media Age," https://ddbcformation.org/mission-statement/

CONCLUSIONS IN AN UNFINISHED TALE

Someone once said, accurately I think, "Forecasting is the art of saying what will happen, and then explaining why it didn't!"[1] and American humorist Leo Rosten quipped, "Some things are so unexpected that no one is prepared for them."[2] That probably has never been truer than in this age of technology-fueled rapid, exponential change. The trouble with sailing an ancient and significant institution like the church today is that our sea is increasingly shallow. That is those whom we seek to lead and whose spiritual lives we seek to shape have significantly less institutional memory or, perhaps, investment. The church plays a diminished and diminishing role in their lives and in the lives of their families. Their faith in God or in things of the Spirit is not shallower, but their investment in Christendom and our religious institutions is certainly less deep.

If present trends continue, the decline in the mainline church's vitality will only accelerate for the immediate future according to research by the Pew Institute:

One of the most important factors in the declining share of Christians and the growth of the "nones" is generational replacement. As the Millennial generation enters adulthood, its members display much

---

[1] Anonymous
,http://www.met.reading.ac.uk/Research/cagold/forecasting/quotes.html

[2] Leo Rosten, *Rome Wasn't Burned in a Day: The Mischief of Language* (New York: Doubleday, 1972)*, 23*

103

lower levels of religious affiliation, including less connection with Christian churches, than older generations. Fully 36% of young Millennials (those between the ages of 18 and 24) are religiously unaffiliated, as are 34% of older Millennials (ages 25-33). And fewer than six-in-ten Millennials identify with any branch of Christianity, compared with seven-in-ten or more among older generations, including Baby Boomers and Gen-Xers. Just 16% of Millennials are Catholic, and only 11% identify with mainline Protestantism.[3]

Although they explore what they call "America's changing religious landscape," I have chosen to describe the setting of our faith as a "shallow sea." The word "landscape" implies a greater stability and predictability than the future generally offers. Storms, like the attacks on September 11, 2001, or the explosion of new technology, or electoral turmoil, can cause significant shifts in the reality in which we seek to function. As we often see in the Gospel stories, winds can shift, and storms can rise rapidly on a shallow sea. Change is the one certainty we carry with us into the future.

It is likely that institutions such as the mainline church will continue to decline. This is not inevitable; however, if history is a predictor, most congregations will not adapt quickly or well to the significant social changes going on around them. As these changes accelerate with the passing of the generation that has provided continuity in most congregations, the impact can be devastating. An optimist might suggest that the opportunities also may be incredible.

We have been given a chance to renew and reclaim what is good, healthy, functional, and life-giving in the church and in our faith. The extent to which we are willing to let go of the traditions that have lost significance for the future will be a major deciding factor. We also must find ways to enliven and reinterpret practices such as worship, service, and spiritual formation so that they can anchor the lives of contemporary seekers without drowning them in meaningless traditions. Congregations

---

[3] "America's Changing Religious Landscape," Pew Research Center, http://www.pewforum.org/2015/05/12/americas-changing-religious-landscape/, (May 12, 2015)

that can adapt to the present seas on which we sail will certainly fare better and may even thrive.

The current state of decline seems to parallel the decline of the church in most of Europe. David Voas of the University College London and Mark Chaves at Duke University authored a paper in which they ask, "Is the United States a Counterexample to the Secularization Thesis?" In brief, their conclusion is, no, it is not:

Virtually every discussion of secularization asserts that high levels of religiosity in the United States make it a decisive counterexample to the claim that modern societies are prone to secularization. Focusing on trends rather than levels, the authors maintain that, for two straightforward empirical reasons, the United States should no longer be considered a counterexample. First, it has recently become clear that American religiosity has been declining for decades. Second, this decline has been produced by the generational patterns underlying religious decline elsewhere in the West: each successive cohort is less religious than the preceding one. America is not an exception.[4]

What makes this and any conclusion suspect, however, is the fact that we live in a day when the very nature of change has changed. It is no longer a linear process with predictable challenges and opportunities. Institutions must shift from *planning* to *preparation*. Plans are a linear attempt to control outcomes moving into the future. With a future as rapidly changing as ours, plans are almost as useless as prognostications. A simple survey of the rate of technological change provides a glimpse into the futility of seeking to plan in a world that is so vastly different even from one year to the next.[5]

---

[4] David Voas and Mark Chaves, "Is the United States a Counterexample to the Secularization Thesis?", *American Journal of Sociology* Volume 121, Number 5 (March 2016), https://www.journals.uchicago.edu/doi/abs/10.1086/684202

[5] Priyanka Maharana, "Technological singularity," *AME News*, http://www.amenews.in/technological-singularity/, (August 12, 2017)

The rate of accelerated social change is so new that it is impossible to ultimately predict how individuals, or cultures, or institutions will respond to continuous change. Some effects, however, already can be observed. Dr. Larry Richard, a psychologist who works with lawyers trying to deal with the stress of accelerated change, writes:

It puts us in a constant state of alert. We remain "off balance" much of the time. Since it has no end point, we're never fully able to relinquish all of our refocused attention. There's always a part of our brain that's vigilant in case the next iteration of change brings with it some more dire consequence.

Much of this heightened threat sensitivity is out of conscious awareness, but most people feel a vague sense of unease. Change – especially change that's been described as continuous, accelerating, disruptive, unrelenting, exponential change – produces uncertainty, which, in turn, triggers the brain's threat response system, thus producing anxiety.

Other effects of this "change-uncertainty-stress" cycle can include:

- *Mood swings and emotional lability*
- *An increase in negative emotions such as irritability, distractibility, sadness, worry, agitation or passivity*
- *A narrowing of one's attention, thus precipitating an increase in errors of omission*
- *A tendency to operate closer to the "worst self" end of our behavioral repertory instead of at the "best self" end of the continuum*
- *A disconnecting from others*
- *Lower levels of trust, increased cynicism.* [6]

---

[6] Larry Richard, "The psychology of coping with change," Thomson Reuters, https://blogs.thomsonreuters.com/answerson/psychology-coping-change/, (September 26, 2016)

Dr. Richard's observations provide a challenging list of ministry opportunities for churches seeking to serve an emotionally- and spiritually-stressed society. On the volatile and tumultuous seas of the 21st century, the church can provide community and connection, meaning and mission, and hope for a future beyond vocational success.

The results of this work are still uncertain. In 2010, the associate conference minister of the Southeast Conference of the United Church of Christ said that Virginia-Highland Church had declined beyond the point of recovery and recommended strongly and confidently that it should be closed. She hoped that the building might be retained by the denomination to use in starting a new, less traditional church. Her conclusion was not unreasonable given that the building needed significant repair, average weekly attendance was below 30, and more than 50 percent of the church's income was from building rentals. The church was unable even to pay the conference minimum salary for a half-time pastor.

While it is premature to draw conclusions, today's Virginia-Highland Church:

- Recently elected their first full-time pastor since 1989,
- Has an extensive homeless ministry that involves more than one-third of the membership in some way, and has received more than $1 million in grants and donations,
- Has a vibrant children's ministry with paid staff,
- Is involved in justice work at the state and local level, advocating especially for the undocumented, homeless, and lesbian, gay, bisexual, and transgender citizens,
- Has a well-branded, clearly-identified, compelling, and universally-embraced mission and vision,
- Attracts a sufficient number of visitors to sustain its future membership,
- Is financially stable, largely due to a comprehensive auto-giving system,
- Provides weekly worship, attracting a diverse congregation that is significantly younger than the national average and is five times the number that attended when this experiment began,

- Has a restored building that is being made accessible to all.

The work I have done consulting and in the classroom is, as yet, impossible to evaluate fully. Anecdotal evidence has been offered repeatedly to support the conclusion that we are on the right track in identifying tools that can help sustain churches sailing in rapidly changing seas. This work in these three settings: local church, consulting with more than a dozen congregations, and teaching students seeking practical skills leads to the conclusion that, ultimately, churches need:

- A clear and compelling externally focused vision and mission rooted in the DNA of the congregation but relevant to the current cultural setting,
- Worship that is passionate and enthusiastic, rooted in traditions of the past, but enlivened with relevancy for the present,
- Spiritual formation that is balanced between reflection and action, and nourished using methodology and technology relevant and available today,
- Congregational management systems that connect people virtually and support the gathering, mobilizing, informing, inspiring, supporting, and caring for the physical community,
- Stewardship that is rooted in spiritual practices of generosity and facilitated by use of current technology,
- And structures and systems that minimize management and maximize ministry, are permission giving, flexible and adaptable, and align with the genuine mission and ministry of the church.

Many of these are vitality principles that congregations could have utilized during the past several decades. What perhaps distinguishes them for our day is the structural agility and technological acumen that churches will need to thrive on the constantly changing sea on which we sail today.

The challenges are great, and many churches, and even denominations, will not survive. However, with the challenges come both cultural needs and ministry opportunities. Shakespeare wrote:

Fishing in a Shallow Sea

There is a tide in the affairs of men.
Which, taken at the flood, leads on to fortune;
Omitted, all the voyage of their life
Is bound in shallows and in miseries.
On such a full sea are we now afloat,
And we must take the current when it serves,
Or lose our ventures.[7]

Now is the time the church must seize the tide or "lose our ventures."

---

[7] William Shakespeare, "Julius Caesar," Act IV, Scene iii

SHALLOW SEA CONSULTATION

Agile Church Consulting began in 2015 after I ended my tenure at the Center for Progressive Renewal. Created to focus on mainline churches, Agile Church Consulting's initial focus was developing technology for small- to medium-sized mainline churches and training them to use it to grow their church. What our original business model failed to appreciate fully was the rate of change in technology, even for churches.

Because there are more than 300,000 local churches in America,[1] major corporations have started targeting their technology products to the church market. Because we could not develop and maintain technology for churches fast enough to be competitive, we decided to focus instead on assessment, teaching, training, and coaching local churches. The template we use is highly adaptable given the varying situations, yet it is remarkable how many churches are struggling with the same issues and how many of these struggles are related to the rapid rate of change that even churches cannot evade.[2]

---

[1] "America's Changing Religious Landscape," Pew Research Center, http://www.pewforum.org/2015/05/12/chapter-1-the-changing-religious-composition-of-the-u-s/, (May 12, 2015)

[2] Rich Birch, "8 Charts That Explain How Our Culture is Changing. (& 24 questions about the impact on your church)," http://www.unseminary.com/8-charts-that-explain-how-our-culture-is-changing-24-questions-about-the-impact-on-your-church/, (July 2, 2014)

Using many of the skills learned and resources gained from my first year in the Hartford Seminary Doctor of Ministry program, we begin our consultation with what we call a "Health Check." This is a comprehensive assessment of the church and the community. Appendices A and B are copies of the typical questions we seek to answer in a Health Check. Appendix C is a sample of the report we provide to a local congregation.

Based on the results, we generally work with the leadership on some of the most pressing issues facing the church:

1. **Stewardship** rapidly has become a hallmark of our consulting practice. Because people attend with decreasing frequency, their money also may attend less often. In this consultation, we work with the church to:

   a. Make the church the "charity of choice." This requires extensive use of technology to track the hours members give to various programs and ministries. If the hours are tracked and then given an objective financial value,[3] the resulting contribution the church makes to the larger community is almost always much greater than the church has appreciated, owned, or publicized.

   b. Leverage the trends away from *giving* and toward *spending.* This is connected to the previous project of making the church the "charity of choice." We try to inform the congregational culture that different generations give for different reasons and then help the church leverage that information.

   c. Use small groups and spiritual disciplines, like observing Lent, to embed *generosity as a spiritual value* and *giving as a spiritual practice* into the life of the congregation. We have several programs that help do this. The most popular

---

[3] "Independent Sector Releases New Value of Volunteer Time of $24.14 Per Hour," Independent Sector, https://independentsector.org/news-post/value-volunteer-time/, (April 20, 2017)

and effective has been what we call "The Micah Project." (See Appendix D)

    d. Shift the energy investment in the church from a traditional pledge campaign to automatic giving. We teach the church to use technology to get at least 70 percent of their congregation signed up for recurring giving. This shift alone generally results in at least a 10 percent increase in giving year over year.

2. The second most frequent need we identify with the church is the lack of clarity of **vision, mission, and values**. The great challenge is not developing a new vision/mission statement; that can be done quickly and easily. The challenge is getting the congregation to self-identify their unique and unifying values and then to articulate a vision and mission that arises from that. Discovering the DNA of a congregation takes time; enabling a congregation to discover and own it for themselves is an even greater challenge.

    To achieve this, we have created an intensive two-year program that dozens of churches have used effectively. The program is called *reVision*. (See Appendix E) The program is absolutely overwhelming for most churches, so we work with them to identify the parts that are essential for their setting.

3. The other area where we have focused much of our attention is combining a "**communication audit**" with a technology consultation. A church's database, or more accurately their CMS (Church Management System), is a major key to successfully navigating church life in a "shallow sea." The priority, of course, is not only finding a system that is effective and affordable, but also one that can be effectively utilized to stay in touch with members, constituents, and visitors. It must:

    a. Track attendance in worship, small groups, and ministries,
    b. Manage and track volunteers,
    c. Facilitate communication while maintaining confidentiality,
    d. Support financial functions, especially electronic and recurring giving, and

    e. Support "virtual spiritual formation."

In addition, we evaluate the church's branding, communication system, website, and more.

A year of intense consultation almost always is followed by a second year in which we work with the church on additional issues, such as staffing or aligning programming with their new vision/mission, or we provide a year of "coaching." By this we mean we are available to answer questions, identify resources, or meet remotely with their leadership for conversations.

Many of these consultations have arisen after a church attends one of our "Vitality Days." These are Saturday sessions with multiple churches in attendance. They generally last from 10 a.m.-3 p.m., are multimedia driven, and present specific and tangible information for local churches on:

- **Worship for Which People Return** (curating 52 transformational worship services a year)
- **Generational Generosity**
- **Speaking Millennial-ese** (communication/evangelism using technology and social media)
- **Whitewater Rafting for Churches** (structures, governance, and systems that enable churches to navigate in the midst of exponential change)

Churches that attend Vitality Days often are overwhelmed by how much the world has changed and discouraged by how ineffectual what they are doing is for a vibrant future. They often emerge wanting a consultation that will solve their problems. That is a formula for failure for both consultant and church. What they really need is a guide who can help them identify their own assets, wisdom, and paths forward. Solutions that come from the outside or "experts" seldom seem to have lasting impact. Helping people discover their own answers, however, can result in long-term change.

COMPREHENSIVE HEALTH CHECK

I t's critically important for all churches to pause regularly to assess their health. It's particularly important to get an outsider's view from someone who can look at how a church is doing compared to other churches of the same size and in a similar setting, and who can offer proven solutions to any challenges that are identified. Skipping regular church checkups is like ignoring your own health until what could have been a minor correction becomes a life-threatening condition.

This is Agile Church's most comprehensive consulting service. Using personal observation, interviews, comparative assessment tools, and other research, we provide a thorough report to church leadership with insights and specific recommendations we believe will generate immediate results to strengthen the church and promote healthy growth.

The Agile Church Comprehensive Heath Check includes a high-level demographic study of the community as well as evaluations of a church's:

- Facility and setting
- Worship
- Vision, mission, and values
- Technology infrastructure
- Website and social media programs
- Communication, marketing, and branding
- Safe Church policy and practices
- Stewardship and development
- Spiritual formation programs
- Governance
- Ministries
- Staffing alignment for critical skill sets
- Volunteer engagement and tracking

Comprehensive Church Health Assessment

Pre-Assessment Documentation

Prior to the church site visit, please forward a copy of the following information to the Agile Church consultant.

☐ Church leadership goals for this assessment

☐ A summary of known challenges, barriers and conflict

☐ All governing documents, policies and procedures

☐ An organizational chart that, in addition to paid staff, includes the committee/governance structure

☐ Any other information you believe might be helpful for the assessment

☐ Church attendance and contribution data (see table below)

	2016	2015	2014	2013	2012
Annual Contribution Budget	$	$	$	$	$
Total Contribution income	$	$	$	$	$
Avg. Weekly Attendance					

Site Assessment

The consultant will write observations of each critical area including but not limited to the specific topics listed below. The final report may be organized in a different (priority) order.

Facility/Setting

☐ Drive-up appeal / First Impression

☐ Signage

☐ Parking

☐ Visible entry points

☐ Relationship to community

Fishing in a Shallow Sea

Worship

- ☐ Seating capacity, style(s), arrangement, etc.

- ☐ Entry Point(s) in relation to seating arrangement

- ☐ Hospitality, first-time visitor process, attendance, follow-up, seeker focus

- ☐ Appearance, lighting and acoustics

- ☐ Chancel arrangement (includes placement of instruments and choir/ensembles/soloists)

- ☐ Media support and quality (Screens, projectors, worship presentation/recording – video/audio)

- ☐ Seeker-friendly worship guide

- ☐ Service pacing, message relevance, inspiring experience, music quality

- ☐ How is the order of worship/liturgy created and reviewed post-service?

Stewardship and Development

- ☐ Income streams and percent of total budget (e.g. contribution, non-contribution, endowments)

- ☐ Program schedule/leadership, role of the pastor, role of the church council or board and relationship to the budget. How are goals established?

- ☐ Spiritual formation program regarding generous living as a spiritual value

- ☐ Collateral support and communication methods (print, pew envelopes, auto/electronic giving pew cards, thank-you notes)

- ☐ Giving Options (e.g. cash, check, text, credit card, kiosk, online, electronic, recurring gifts)

- ☐ Endowment or program development funding programs

- ☐ How does the church celebrate success?

Michael S. Piazza

Volunteer Engagement

☐ Volunteer recruitment, participation and evaluation process

☐ Percent of members/friends of the church engaged in a volunteer ministry

☐ External vs. Internal focus

☐ Church sponsored opportunities or through partner organizations (are contributions direct or through the church?)

☐ Is individual volunteer participation tracked?

Spiritual Formation

☐ Percent of members/friends of the church engaged in a small group study/spiritual conversation

☐ Percent participating in traditional Sunday-school classes (tracking success?)

☐ On-site vs. Off-site, variable scheduling

☐ Age groups included (any college-age programs)

☐ Curriculum internally created or externally sourced. How topical and relevant to present environment and audience

Evangelism/Marketing/Branding

☐ Community perception or reputation of the church. What is the church known for in the community?

☐ Who does the congregation believe is the "customer" (themselves or seekers)?

☐ Well-defined target market and an understanding of their expectations

☐ Social media program, preferences, drivers. Encouraged during worship?

☐ Website review and pervasiveness of logo, web/social media URL, vision/mission

☐ Attendance, first-time visitor (FTV) tracking database. Timely response to FTV

☐ Weekly communication tools (email, social-media posts, texts)

Mission/Vision/Values

☐ Compelling and Inspirational

☐ When developed? Achieved or still a relevant challenge in contemporary culture?

☐ Can members easily share who the church is (Vision) and what they do (Mission) with visitors or friends?

☐ Integrated into church culture, marketing, and decision making

☐ Movement toward vision is measurable and reported

☐ Mission achievements are regularly celebrated

MICAH PROJECT OVERVIEW

T*he Micah Project* is designed to leverage a congregation's spiritual health and vitality. As a church that does many things well, it will require incredible discipline to spend even 40 days with a singular focus, yet the power of that laser focus has the potential to be transformational. For the 40 days of Lent, the passion and energy of the entire program and ministry of the church will seek to:

- Do justice,
- Love mercy, and
- Walk humbly with God. (Micah 6:8)

This is what the prophet Micah said was "required" of us, and we will earnestly seek as a community of faith to fulfill that requirement with all our heart, soul, mind, and strength for the 40 days of Lent.

On Transfiguration Sunday and Ash Wednesday, we will invite every member of the church to enter into a covenant to join the Micah Project for 40 days. In doing so, they will promise to:

1. **Do justice.** By this we mean that they will seek to find a way to do some act of justice every day. This may be as simple as sending an email to their senator or city council person. They may want to post something on Facebook or challenge a racist comment or pray that their company or their state will change an unjust policy. The church will also try to identify weekly activities that gather members together to "do justice." This may be classes on social activism, or letter-writing parties, or bringing in speakers, or

joining protests. South American Bishop and activist Dom Helder Camera once wrote, "When I give bread to the poor, they call me a saint. When I ask why people are poor, they call me a communist." The job of the church is to care for those in need AND address the systems that create so many needy people.

2. **Love mercy.** During Lent, we also ask every member to do an act of mercy every day. It can be as simple as putting money in a parking meter that is expired or paying for the groceries of the single mother in line behind them. The church also should be mobilized to do weekly projects of mercy. In a large congregation there may need to be several opportunities each week. Some may be ongoing projects that happen all Lent long, and others may be one time. Some may be specifically designed to get youth or children involved, and some simply may be child-friendly. All should include an awareness of why we are doing this and an invitation to surround the action with a spirit or prayerful awareness that we are both serving and being served.

3. **Walk humbly with God.** Here, too, we ask people to do this in three very specific ways:
    a. **Worship every week**. If they are out of town, worship where they are or attend an alternative worship service, or at least participate in a service online.
    b. **Join a small group**. The small groups will be studying the Micah Project and the entire congregation will be taking this Lenten journey to Easter together.
    c. **Tithe**. Yes, this is a different prophet—Malachi, not Micah—but, because financial generosity is the most challenging spiritual discipline, we are asking everyone to give it a try for the next 40 days. The promise of Malachi is that if we will God will "open the windows of heaven." We anticipate that if we are faithful Easter morning will find us with our faces turned heavenward to the sunrise of God's eternal love.

These are very specific practices, and though we will talk about them during Lent and study them in our small groups, we must lay the groundwork for them during Epiphany. The staff and lay leadership must begin to build a sense of anticipation about Lent/Easter on the first Sunday of the year so people are ready to engage this spiritual adventure.

Transfiguration Sunday needs to be well attended so as many people as possible will be present to sign their "Micah Covenant" cards. You may want to celebrate Mardi Gras Sunday with balloons, king cake, pancakes, beads, etc. The sermon on that Sunday needs to talk specifically about what we are asking people to do and challenge them to give it a try. This is a Sunday to be direct (pointed) not an occasion for congregational/mid-western ambiguity or politeness. The specificity of this program is what gives it power and in the end it is what millennials love most about it.

The **spiritual formation/Christian education** people need to recruit and train small group leaders as soon as possible. It would be great to have two leaders for every group. They need at least eight-10 people in each group and never more than 16-18. We will need groups that meet at different times and in different locations. We will also need groups for different age groups. The leaders need to be on-board with the idea of personally committing during Lent. They have to lead with integrity if this is going to work.

The **communication team** needs to be prepared to promote Lent as soon as the Advent wreath comes down. It happens very quickly, so all this needs to be planned before Christmas. Covenant cards need to be designed. Mailings, both electronic and snail, need to be prepared. Everyone should get a Lenten mailing inviting/urging their participation two weeks before Ash Wednesday.

The **music/worship team** should be asked to join the effort to make each of the services as deeply moving as possible. This may challenge us to get out of the box and find some ways to be creative. Is it possible to offer an opportunity to respond in each service during Lent: bring a covenant card forward, light a candle, take communion, wash a neighbor's hands, take a stone/pocket cross/saint card. The idea is to do something with each Sunday that will allow people to say a couple of years from now, "Remember that Sunday when we …."

The major role of the **generosity team** during this time is to ensure that ALL the teams are on board. This may mean having a team member go to them and ask them personally to help make this Lent the most transformational season in the life of the church:

This is a Holy Experiment and we need your help. We are asking everyone, in particular leaders like you, to engage a set of specific spiritual practices for 40 days. We can do most anything for 40 days, but the Bible seems to imply that this is a long enough season to transform our lives. We want to take that seriously and see what a difference it might make in the life of our church. Will you help us? We can't ask the members to do something our leaders won't do so we are starting by asking you.

The idea, of course, is that by the time you get all of the teams to commit, between them and their spouses, you probably will have a couple hundred people already on board. This greatly increases the likelihood that this will have a powerful impact on the life of the church.

FINAL REFLECTIONS

As of this writing, the United Church of Christ has 113 positions open for fulltime pastors and 84 for part-time pastors. As attendance and giving continue to diminish, those numbers inevitably will trade places. When I became a student pastor more than four decades ago, the United Methodist Church guaranteed every church a pastor and every pastor a fulltime position. Indeed, the shortage of clergy in my home conference is what forced them to recruit a 19-year-old to pastor three rural churches. As times have changed, the Methodists have had to change those policies. If current trends continue, pastoral ministry soon will be a part-time vocation.

Partly because of this trend, I have spent the past several years working as consultant, technology entrepreneur, professor, and author to pay for my pastoral "habit." The frustration has been that the work of leading a vital congregation has become more and more difficult during this time. Having an impact on traditional metrics of success—attendance, membership, and giving—has required much more effort simply to ensure the church does not decline. It has been my good fortune that the work that actually paid my bills also afforded me the opportunity to learn new technological skills for which my pastoral ministry was desperate. In addition, working on this project forced me to reflect on what I was doing and to attend to the impact when what I thought was true was applied.

By most standards, my pastoral career is considered a success. When the United Church of Christ asked me to begin sharing what I know about growing mainline churches, I realized that I actually did not know what I knew. For my entire career, I have attended conferences, taken classes and workshops, and read almost every book about thriving churches and businesses. I was fortunate to have mentors like Robert Schuller, Lyle Schaller, and Fred Craddock, who are largely responsible for any success I've known. This project, along with taking classes at Austin Presbyterian and Hartford Seminaries, has forced me to reflect on what works and does not work in ministry and why.

Michael S. Piazza

President John F. Kennedy once referenced a story by Irish writer Frank O'Connor while speaking in 1963 about his commitment to space exploration despite the dangers and many unknown factors. He explained how O'Connor and his friends "would make their way across the countryside, and when they came to an orchard wall that seemed too high and too difficult to permit their voyage to continue, they took off their hats and tossed them over the wall—and then they had no choice but to follow them." Kennedy then applied this to the nation and declared that the United States had "tossed its cap over the wall of space, and we have no choice but to follow it."[1] That describes much of my ministry, teaching, consulting, and writing.

During recent years, I have taught 10 classes at Hartford Seminary. I previously had taught only one of them. I usually turned in a class topic and then began reading and doing research to discover if I actually understood what I wanted to teach and had the facts to support it. This project is a collection of much of that learning and its application at Virginia-Highland Church, in a graduate course, and in a successful consulting practice. We speak of physicians "practicing" medicine. I believe this is true of doctors of ministry, too. Remembering that keeps us agile and adaptable, which is vital for meaningful and effective ministry on a shallow sea. The only thing of which I am certain is that this project is just one more step in a process of learning to practice ministry that I'm only now learning to do with a modicum of conscious competency.

I am deeply grateful to my colleagues, professors, and mentors at Hartford Seminary for the privilege to learn among them. I owe a special debt of gratitude to Rev. Dr. Donna Schaper and to the indefatigable Dr. Scott Thumma, who is the one who threw my hat over the Doctor of Ministry wall. Then he used his considerable strength to boost me over as well.

I also must say thanks to my long-time partner in ministry David Plunkett who has edited most of my writings since 2002 and has kept me from embarrassing myself. He deserves a great deal of credit for this work.

---

[1] John F. Kennedy, "Remarks at the Dedication of the Aerospace Medical Health Center, San Antonio, Texas," https://www.jfklibrary.org/Research/Research-Aids/JFK-Speeches/San-Antonio-TX_19631121.aspx, (November 21, 1963)

And to my dear Bill Eure … At the end of my first semester at Hartford we celebrated our 35th anniversary. A few weeks later, we learned he had stage four abdominal cancer. We spent the second semester being deeply tested by doctors and chemotherapy. He was determined that I not stop on his account. He and David accompanied me to Hartford in June of 2016, and, while I taught "Worship and Preaching that Grows Churches" (AM-627), they were tourists in Hartford and in New York City where they saw "Hamilton" with the original cast. He then sat in the back of my final class on Friday to see what I did and where I did it. Bill died a month later. The fact that he is not here to see this adventure's completion is my only regret because, more than anyone on earth, it is to him I owe the most profound and abiding debt of gratitude.

BIBLIOGRAPHY

Alper, Becka A. "Millennials are less religious than older Americans, but just as spiritual." November 23, 2015. <http://www.pewresearch.org/fact-tank/2015/11/23/millennials-are-less-religious-than-older-americans-but-just-as-spiritual/>.

American Psychological Association. "The Road to Resilience." <http://www.apa.org/helpcenter/road-resilience.aspx>.

Birch, Rich. "8 Charts That Explain How Our Culture is Changing. (& 24 questions about the impact on your church)." July 2, 2014. <http://www.unseminary.com/8-charts-that-explain-how-our-culture-is-changing-24-questions-about-the-impact-on-your-church/>.

Bourque, Andre, "Are Millennials the Most Generous Generation?" March 29, 2016 <https://www.entrepreneur.com/article/271466>.

Conerly, Bill. "The Death of Strategic Planning: Why?" March 24, 2014. <https://www.forbes.com/forbes/welcome/?toURL=https://www.forbes.com/sites/billconerly/2014/03/24/the-death-of-strategic-planning-why/&refURL>.

Conner, Daryl R. *Managing at the Speed of Change: How Resilient Managers Succeed and Prosper Where Others Fail*. New York: Random House, 1999.

Daly, Mary. *Beyond God the Father: Toward a Philosophy of Women's Liberation*. Boston: Beacon Press, 1985.

Dashnaw, Cindy. "The Millennial Impact Report: Phase 1: Millennial Dialogue on the Landscape of Cause Engagement and Social Issues." p.

8
<http://www.themillennialimpact.com/sites/default/files/reports/Phase1
Report_MIR2017_060217.pdf>.

de Bono, Edward. *I am Right and You are Wrong: From This to the New Renaissance: From Rock Logic to Water Logic*. London: Penguin Books, 1991.

"Digital Discipleship: Lifelong Learners in the New Media Age." <https://ddbcformation.org/mission-statement/>.

Dyck, Drew. "Explainer: Ancient-Future Worship." 2009. <http://www.christianitytoday.com/pastors/2009/may-online-only/explainer-ancient-future-worship.html>.

Easum, Bill. *Sacred Cows Make Gourmet Burgers: Ministry Anytime, Anywhere, By Anyone*. Nashville: Abingdon Press, 1995.

Evans, Rachel Held. "Want millennials back in the pews? Stop trying to make church 'cool.'." April 30. 2015. <https://www.washingtonpost.com/opinions/jesus-doesnt-tweet/2015/04/30/fb07ef1a-ed01-11e4-8666-a1d756d0218e_story.html?utm_term=.f95bb60cecaa>.

Exoo, George. "GOD'S Country." D Magazine. (September 1997) <https://www.dmagazine.com/publications/d-magazine/1997/september/gods-country/>.

Finke, Roger and Rodney Stark. *The Churching of America, 1776-1990*. New Jersey: Rutgers University Press, 1992

Flory, Richard and Donald Miller. *Finding Faith: The Spiritual Quest of the Post-Boomer Generation*. New Brunswick, NJ: Rutgers University Press, 2008.

Foss, Michael W. *Power Surge: Six Marks Of Discipleship For A Changing Church*. Minneapolis: Fortress Press, 2000.

Frey, William H. "Diversity defines the millennial generation." June 28, 2016. <https://www.brookings.edu/blog/the-avenue/2016/06/28/diversity-defines-the-millennial-generation/>.

Hadaway, C. Kirk. *Behold I Do a New Thing: Transforming Communities of Faith*. Bohemia, New York, 2001.

Harward, Doug. "Innovation in Educational Planning." <u>Training Industry</u> Volume 10, Issue 1 (Nov./Dec. 2016) p.28. <https://www.trainingindustry.com/magazine/nov-dec-2016/key-trends-for-2017-innovation-in-educational-technology/>.

Heckert, Amanda, ed. "Hot 'Hoods." <u>Atlanta Magazine</u>. (June 2011) <https://web.archive.org/web/20110930085606/http://www.atlantamagazine.com/features/neighborhoods/home.aspx>.

Herrington, Jim; Mike Bonem; and James H. Furr. *Leading Congregational Change: A Practical Guide for the Transformational Journey*. San Francisco: Jossey-Bass, 2000.

Hoffer, Eric. *Reflections on the Human Condition*. New York City: Harper & Row, 1973.

Independent Sector. "Independent Sector Releases New Value of Volunteer Time of $24.14 Per Hour." April 20, 2017. <https://independentsector.org/news-post/value-volunteer-time/>.

Johnston, Will. "Clearing the Way for Small Groups." February 22, 2016. <http://www.smallgroups.com/articles/2016/clearing-way-for-small-groups.html>.

Kennedy, John F. "Remarks at the Dedication of the Aerospace Medical Health Center, San Antonio, Texas." November 21, 1963.

https://www.jfklibrary.org/Research/Research-Aids/JFK-Speeches/San-Antonio-TX_19631121.aspx,

Koch, Richard. *The 80/20 Principle: The Secret to Achieving More with Less*. New York: Doubleday, 2008.

Konnikova, Maria. "How People Learn to Become Resilient." February 11, 2016. <https://www.newyorker.com/science/maria-konnikova/the-secret-formula-for-resilience>.

Kotter, John P. *Leading Change*. Watertown, Massachusetts: Harvard Business Review Press, 1996.

Lakoff, George. *The ALL NEW Don't Think of an Elephant!: Know Your Values and Frame the Debate*. White River Junction, Vermont: Chelsea Green Publishing, 2014.

Lipka, Michael. "A closer look at America's rapidly growing religious 'nones'." May 13, 2005. <http://www.pewresearch.org/fact-tank/2015/05/13/a-closer-look-at-americas-rapidly-growing-religious-nones/>.

_____. "Which U.S. religious groups are oldest and youngest?" July 11, 2016 <http://www.pewresearch.org/fact-tank/2016/07/11/which-u-s-religious-groups-are-oldest-and-youngest>.

Lyons, Linda. "Tracking U.S. Religious Preferences Over the Decades." May 24, 2005. <http://news.gallup.com/poll/16459/tracking-us-religious-preferences-over-decades.aspx>.

McCraken, Brent. *Uncomfortable: The Awkward and Essential Challenge of Christian Community*. Wheaton, IL: Crossway, 2017.

McFee, Marcia. "Flatlining - Worship Vitality Killers." <https://www.youtube.com/watch?v=CsvxeW-d9DQ>.

McNeal, Reggie. *Missional Renaissance: Changing the Scorecard for the Church*. San Francisco: Jossey-Bass, 2009.

Newport, Frank. "Five Key Findings on Religion in the U.S." December 23, 2016. <http://news.gallup.com/poll/200186/five-key-findings-religion.aspx>.

Newton, Casey. "How one of the best films at Sundance was shot using an iPhone 5S." January 28, 2015. <https://www.theverge.com/2015/1/28/7925023/sundance-film-festival-2015-tangerine-iphone-5s>.

Newton, Isaac. "Newton's First Law." <http://www.physicsclassroom.com/class/newtlaws/Lesson-1/Newton-s-First-Law>.

O'Donovan, Dana and Noah Rimland Flower. "The Strategic Plan is Dead. Long Live Strategy." Stanford Social Innovation Review, (January 10, 2013). <https://ssir.org/articles/entry/the_strategic_plan_is_dead._long_live_strategy>.

Overholt, Alison. "Do You Hear What Starbucks Hears?" July 1, 2004. <https://www.fastcompany.com/50607/do-you-hear-what-starbucks-hears>.

Pava, Calvin. "New Strategies of Systems Change: Reclaiming Nonsynoptic Methods." July 1, 1986. <http://journals.sagepub.com/doi/abs/10.1177/001872678603900702>.

Peck, M. Scott. *A World Waiting to Be Born: Civility Rediscovered*. New York: Bantam Books, 1993.

Peck, M. Scott. *The Different Drum: Community Making and Peace*. New York: Touchstone, 1987.

Pew Research Center. "America's Changing Religious Landscape." May 12, 2015. <http://www.pewforum.org/2015/05/12/chapter-1-the-changing-religious-composition-of-the-u-s/>.

_____. "Religious Landscape Study: Attendance at religious services." <http://www.pewforum.org/religious-landscape-study/attendance-at-religious-services/>.

Priyanka Maharana, "Technological singularity." August 12, 2017. <http://www.amenews.in/technological-singularity/>.

"Psychological resilience." <https://en.wikipedia.org/wiki/Psychological_resilience>.

Rainer, Thom S. "The Number One Reason for the Decline in Church Attendance and Five Ways to Address It." August 19, 2013. <http://thomrainer.com/2013/08/the-number-one-reason-for-the-decline-in-church-attendance-and-five-ways-to-address-it/>.

"Recurring Giving: A Game Changer for Churches." February 27, 2017. <http://blog.easytithe.com/recurring-giving/>.

Reese, Martha Grace Reese. *Unbinding the Gospel: Real Life Evangelism 2nd Edition*. St. Louis: Chalice Press, 2008.

Rendle, Gil. *Journey Into the Wilderness: New Life for Mainline Churches*. Nashville: Abingdon Press, 2010.

Richard, Larry. "The psychology of coping with change." September 26, 2016. <https://blogs.thomsonreuters.com/answerson/psychology-coping-change/>.

Roberto, John. "Research-based Practices for Shaping Faith Formation across the Life Span." p. 4

<https://www.lifelongfaith.com/uploads/5/1/6/4/5164069/__ctr_for_con gregations_-_research-based_practices_handout.pdf>.

Rosten, Leo. *Rome Wasn't Burned in a Day: The Mischief of Language.* New York: Doubleday, 1972.

Royle, Marjorie H. "Facts on Worship 2010." p.14. <http://faithcommunitiestoday.org/sites/default/files/FACTs-on-Worship.pdf>.

Rusaw, Rick and Eric Swanson. *The Externally Focused Church.* Loveland, CO: Group Publishing, 2004.

Seligman, Martin E. P. *Learned Optimism: How to Change Your Mind and Your Life.* New York: Vintage Books, 2006.

Senge, Peter. *The Fifth Discipline: The Art & Practice of The Learning Organization.* New York: Doubleday, 1990.

Shakespeare, William. "Julius Caesar."

Shattuck, Kelly. "7 Startling Facts: An Up Close Look at Church Attendance in America." December 14, 2017. <https://churchleaders.com/pastors/pastor-articles/139575-7-startling-facts-an-up-close-look-at-church-attendance-in-america.html>.

Social Media Chaplaincy Corps. <http://socialmediachaplaincycorp.blogspot.com/p/hurchwide-spiritual-formation-program.html>.

Stetzer, Ed; Richie Stanley; and Jason Hayes. *Lost and Found: The Younger Unchurched and the Churches that Reach Them.* Nashville: B&H Publishing Group, 2009.

The Bible. International Standard Version.

The Bible. New Revised Standard Version.10:16 ISV.

"The Majority of Children Live With Two Parents, Census Bureau Reports." November 17, 2016. <https://www.census.gov/newsroom/press-releases/2016/cb16-192.html>.

UBA Staff. "Bookbrief: Lost and Found: The Younger Unchurched and the Churches That Reach Them." <http://www.ubahouston.org/resources/media/book-notes/lost-and-found--the-younger-unchurched>.

Voas, David and Mark Chaves. "Is the United States a Counterexample to the Secularization Thesis?" American Journal of Sociology Volume 121, Number 5 (March 2016). <https://www.journals.uchicago.edu/doi/abs/10.1086/684202>.

Webber, Robert and Lester Ruth. *Evangelicals on the Canterbury Trail: Why Evangelicals Are Attracted to the Liturgical Church*. New York: Morehouse Publishing, 1985.

Made in the USA
Columbia, SC
10 June 2019